A VERY LARGE ARRAY

JENA OSMAN
A VERY LARGE ARRAY
: SELECTED POEMS

DABA
New York

A VERY LARGE ARRAY

AN ARRAY OF HISTORY

AN
ARRAY
OF
NEWS

AN
ARRAY
OF
SCIENCE

SUPREME COURT ARRAY

THEATER ARRAY

AN ARRAY OF HISTORY

TARGET

TWISTER I

The march. It seems to be moving through the main streets. It seems to be moving like a body made of parts. It seems to be turning and it seems to be coursing and it seems to have a mind of its own. Waking up in the morning in the sheets, then fanning out in determination or panic. Following orders in the heat. Twisting through the terrain. Exploding. Past the tanks. Past the flak jacket. Up and into the brain.

PSYOPS: KNOW YOUR TARGET I

remove any trace of the color red
show soldiers with chin beards rather than clean-shaven faces
don't use thought bubbles; they're confusing
add bananas to a bowl of fruit

LEAFLET I

reward for information
aerial dissemination and arc light operations
the grief and pain of your death
a dog of nomads, chained at the heel
arty artillery
playing chess connects with the target
we know where you are hiding
person to person without distortion
unless physically altered
unexploded ordinance can kill! do not touch! Help us keep
  you safe!
you are our targets
there is no reason to be alarmed. For your own safety,
  stay away!

PSYOPS: KNOW YOUR TARGET II

Keep in mind that the target is suspicious
and will look for hidden unfavorable meanings,
insure that only one interpretation, the intended one, can be given each sentence.
Do not leave any thoughts for the target to fill in.

caption everything

LEAFLET II

safe conduct passes
foreign henchmen
Stop! Turn away now!
rid yourselves of these fanatics
positive appeals wear the target down
Help us keep you safe
read the message without touching
you can receive millions of dollars
the color of the terrain
laughs at you
you do not know he's sent you to your death
many threads make one rug
get wealth and power beyond your dreams
help bring back happiness
millions of dollars selling evil drugs
the audience often risks death for reading
your escape routes are mined
air delivery
you are trapped
the murderer and coward has abandoned you
give yourself up and do not die needlessly
you mean nothing to him
do you think you are safe
in your tomb
we know where you are
stop fighting and live

TWISTER II

The market or target seems to be moving. It seems to be turning and it seems to be declining and it seems to be tied to emotional life. More than one million seem to have moved, displaced, and then hundreds of thousands move with no face. Up into the mountains, in pockets and caves. The borders and barricades. Ticker tape as mechanical echo falling in small twists from above. Something pressing, something pushing, something running from the marksman.

THE JOKER

In medieval times, the joker was misfitting. Physical or mental differences kept him on the sidelines of cultural norms; his role was to play the outsider, the one not held to rules of decorum. In the king's court, only the jester could openly criticize the king (some might say only the jester was allowed to speak truth) and this is why, in the card games that make use of them, jokers always trump the high values of the royals in the pack. They wreak havoc on business as usual.

Sugars.

The theater director Augusto Boal created a "Joker System" as part of his Theater of the Oppressed. As with the court jester, Boal's joker has social flexibility: he can jump in and out of a performance—taking on a variety of roles, asking the audience for criticisms and suggestions for revision. He can comment on the king's law—the authored principles seemingly carved in stone—and suggest that such legislation be rewritten.

Sugars all not above.

The joker is not always so noble. By definition he is unknowable and unpredictable. A wild card. A hidden clause in an otherwise transparent law:

> *1904* N.Y. Even. Post *11 May 1 They are all nervous over the possibility that there may be a hitherto unperceived joker in the present bill. 1914 S. H. ADAMS* Clarion *241 Even her simple mind grasped the joker in the contract. 1928* Daily Express *17 July 8/2 The surtax was slipped into the Finance Act of 1927 very much as a 'joker' is occasionally insinuated into an American Tariff Act—that is to say, surreptitiously, without anybody except those in the know being aware of the significance of what was happening.*

1897. Sugars, all not above No. 16 Dutch
standard in color

tank bottoms, sugar drainings, and sugar
sweepings, sirups of cane juice, melada,
concentrated melada, concrete and
concentrated molasses.

this joker keeps out the light-colored
sugar. a secret pact in (re)finery.

The Philadelphia Mummers parade takes place every New Year's Day. The tradition goes back to the 1700s, with vague connections to the 18th century Mummers plays performed in the streets, house-to-house in England. After the Civil War, the Philadelphia parade became a regularly organized phenomenon, and gained official city sponsorship in 1901. Today's Mummers parades feature about 15,000 participants who march, perform, and strut for two miles over the course of eight hours. They are divided into three divisions: the Comics, the Fancies, and the String Bands.

Sugars.

It is said that the Comics divisions take their cues from Momus—the Greek god of satire, mockery, and criticism. Momus' jabs at the all-powerful gods ultimately got him kicked off Olympus. Similarly, the chaotic Philadelphia Comics have caused their share of controversy by their portrayals of current events, political figures, and racial stereotypes. In 1947 there was an out-right ban of political content for the Comics. In 1964, the city-mandated ban on blackface met with serious resistance from parade participants. And although blackface has been replaced by multi-colored layers of face paint, the shadow of minstrelsy is still very much present: since the early 20th century, the theme song of the parade has been "Oh Dem

Golden Slippers" by the minstrel show composer James Bland, and the famous Mummers' strut that accompanies it is often described as a "cake-walk."

Sugars all not above.

The phrase "cake-walk" came into being somewhere between 1860 and 1865, used to describe dances by enslaved people for their enslavers, who would reward the winner with a slice of cake. Accounts by former enslaved people, told to WPA researchers in the 1930s, indicate that these dances originated as satirical reproductions of the white ballroom dances of the times—but it didn't take long for the direction of the satire to reverse.

Sugars, all not above No. 16 Dutch
standard in color

In 1866, the first all-black Mummers club was founded. But as with the participation of blacks in Congress during Reconstruction, that presence didn't last. There has been almost no African American involvement in the parade since 1929.

And sugar.

For the most part, the Comics of the 2007 parade seemed more interested in fun than politics; pirates, beachgoers, and an assortment of toy trains predominated. However, there were a few soft political targets. The Happy Tappers group sported sombreros and fake guitars while strutting around a portable taco stand with a sign saying "No Espanol, No Tacos." This was a response to an incident the previous June when Geno's Cheesesteaks (a South Philadelphia landmark) posted a sign that said "This Is AMERICA: WHEN ORDERING 'SPEAK

ENGLISH.'" The owner of the cheesesteak stand (son of immigrants himself), said he was trying to encourage immigrants to assimilate.

Dutch standard in color. Twenty
glass bottles.

The sign was broadly condemned, locally and nationally. But was further critique in mind when a brigade of white men chose to caricature Mexicans and march up Broad Street? South Philadelphia—home to the Mummers parade and the generations of white working-class families who participate in it—is in the midst of a powerful transformation. Its newest immigrant classes (mostly Latino and Asian) have taken over much of the residential and commercial space in the area. It's safe to say that the Happy Tappers weren't necessarily celebrating that fact in their 2007 routine.

Sugars, all not above No. 16 Dutch
standard in color.

i.e. not white.

and thus subject to refining

20 glass bottles graded in color

On its best behavior, satire can hold stupidity up to ridicule, imprudence up to scorn. It can expose, denounce, deride. But its defining characteristic is its duplicity, its ability to say one thing while really meaning another. Satire is a double-speaker, a face that wears a mask. The joker might sport a terrific smile, but his interior is deadly serious. In the audience, there's always the fear of not quite getting the joke. Or of being the joker's target. You want to trust, but you feel uncomfortably on edge.

Sugars not above No. 16 Dutch standard
  in color.
tank bottoms
sirups of cane juice
testing by the polariscope not above
  75 degrees
95/100 of 1 cent per pound
1.95/100 cents per pound on sugar above
  No. 16 Dutch standard in color
Beet
Beet (if bounty is paid . . .
Cane
Cane (if bounty is paid . . .

In 1869, while in exile, Victor Hugo published the novel *L'Homme Qui Rit* (*The Man Who Laughs*). The action of the novel takes place sometime in the 17th century. The infant son of an exiled nobleman is sold off by the king to a band of "child sellers" who then carve his face into a permanent smile so as to provide them with entertainment. Eventually abandoned by his mutilators, Gwynplaine makes his living at carnivals and freakshows, keeping his face veiled until the inevitable punchline: the revelation of his grotesquely petrified mouth. Gwynplaine's fortunes seem to reverse when a change in government leads to the reinstatement of his family name and he is made a Lord in parliament; however, laughter and snickers are the only responses his attempts at governing elicit. Not surprisingly, the epic journey of Gywnplaine does not end well. He gives up his seat in despair. Upon his return home, his true love (a blind good-hearted girl whose life he saved in infancy) dies. In response he kills himself by drowning.

Before the dark sugar is put on the
American table,
it must go to a refinery to be whitened.

Although Hugo's novel is now considered one of his more obscure works, Mark Twain almost instantly appropriated it on publication in order to satire the presidency of Andrew Johnson. Hugo's story—which was an allegory for the corrupted state of the aristocracy of Second Empire France—became an allegory for Johnson's inability to compromise during Reconstruction. But in this version of the story, Gwynplaine (Johnson), is not particularly sympathetic. No longer the tragic victim of power gone awry, Gwynplaine now is a perpetrator of vengeance. Once restored to his seat of power, he forgets his good-hearted beginnings and goals.

Sugar trust.

Andrew Johnson was the only Southern Democrat not to quit Congress after Secession. His token status led him to be chosen as Lincoln's Vice President—a symbol of the Union that needed to take place after the Civil War. Upon Lincoln's assassination, he became President. His true feelings about Reconstruction turned out to be ambivalent at best; he vetoed the first Civil Rights bill and tried to block passage of the 14th Amendment. As a result, he was the first president ever to be impeached (although later acquitted) and he lost re-election by a landslide. Unlike the original Gwynplaine, he could not accept that Congress would only laugh at him and the frozen rictus of his opinions. They wanted him to be double—South on the surface, but North underneath—and he would not play it that way.

The light-colored sugar.

Mark Twain, on the other hand, seemed more comfortable in the double role. He had close ties with a number of Southern Democrat politicians, but he was also quite chummy with the publisher of the *Cleveland Herald*, a Radical Republican Newspaper. Although he lived in the North, he dressed the part of the Southern gentleman. His writings were critical of high society, and yet that was where he circulated socially. Twain was good friends with both Nikola Tesla (the visionary and anti-corporate scientist who devoted much of his career to the creation of a time machine) *and* Henry Rogers (the robber baron of Standard Oil). To whom did his sympathies truly belong? The censorship history of Twain's *Huckleberry Finn* further demonstrates the complexity of his stances. Mark Twain was a satirist—but what kind of joke was he telling? Satire always has a target—but when context changes, the target moves. In order to function, must satire be bound to a set of frozen particulars?

MR. FORDNEY. Is not that the law? I beg to differ from you.
MR. BASS. You will not differ from me when you read your own tariff law.

The original title of Hugo's novel was *By Order of the King*, but Hugo discarded it because it seemed to overstate the novel's critique of the aristocracy. Renaming it *The Man Who Laughs*, switched the focus from the ruling class itself to the hideous deformations it produces. Whereas the "misfit" once found safety in serving the king's court as jester, in Hugo's world the ruling class was in the business of deliberately deforming its subjects to its own specifications. Instead of having the power to criticize the king with statements of truth, now the joker had a more limited set of options. His performance becomes one of extreme and dangerous alienation:

> *His face laughed; his thoughts did not. The extraordinary face which chance or a special and weird industry had fashioned for him laughed alone. Gwynplaine had nothing to do with it. The outside did not depend on the interior.*

In 1928 Hugo's novel was made into the Hollywood film *The Man Who Laughs*, starring Konrad Veidt (a German actor better known for his starring role in *The Cabinet of Dr. Caligari*). Directed by another German refugee, Paul Leni, the film was made in a decidedly Expressionist style—a style where the interior regions of the psyche are made concrete by the physical set. The outside *is* the inside. Even so, the Hugo story is re-written with a happy Hollywood ending. Veidt, as Gwynplaine, had to wear a device to pull back his lips and reveal his teeth. He could only use the top half of his face in order to communicate emotion, which meant that the bottom and top halves of his face could send completely contradictory information.

MR. FORDNEY. Is it not 3 ½ cents per 100 pounds on each degree above 96 sugar?
MR. BASS. No sir; that is conditional. It is providing it is not lighter than 16 Dutch standard in color, and then that clause applies, but that is a condition it is

impossible to attain. There is the trickery. That is the joker.

In 1940, a supervillain with an insane grin first appeared in the comic *The Batman*. His victims, usually poisoned by "joker venom," would literally die of laughter.

Or sugar.

Apparently the Joker's appearance (weird hair and skin, a face stretched taut by a frozen smile) was the result of a fall into a vat of chemical waste. Although his grin stayed frozen, his personality shifted during the life of the series. At the start he was a brutal killer. But then it was decided that continuing characters should not be allowed to get away with murder, as this would show Batman to be incompetent. So the Joker became an annoying goofball and practically disappeared by the 1960s. In the 1970s, the Joker came back with a psychopathic vengeance, wielding weapons such as razor-sharp playing cards, electric joy buzzers, and acid-spewing flowers. Part of the horror of his character is that he continues to change with the times, reflecting history as he swings from nose-blowing buffoon to war-mongering avenger.

THE CHAIRMAN. Why is that? Is it prejudice?
MR. WILLETT. The country is demanding better sugar.
THE CHAIRMAN. Are the white sugars much better than the brown sugars, much healthier, or anything like that?
MR. WILLETT. Which white sugars?*

Thirty years after the Joker's first appearance, Batman's creator Bob Kane finally acknowledged his debt to Hugo (by way of Veidt). The 2005 comic book *Batman: The Man Who Laughs* makes the connection explicit.

*The 1912 Congressional hearings held to investigate the monopoly powers of the American Sugar Refining Company questioned the legislative joker that—in the name of "purity"—caused imported sugars white in color (above No. 16 Dutch standard color) to pay a prohibitively high tariff. This tax led importers (particularly Cuba) to trade raw sugars only, which then had to be processed in an American refinery which then controlled the price. Representative Thomas Hardwick, chairman of the proceedings, stated the following:

> The contention has been made before this committee that if the Dutch standard were eliminated from our tariff laws that brown sugars, sugars that are not as white as our granulated sugar by the bone-black process, but are just as good, just as healthy and just as useful, would come in and could be sold to the people at a very much cheaper price; and that that is happening everywhere else in the world except here, and for that reason the retention of the Dutch standard is a hardship upon the poor people of this country.

Science had proven that the Dutch color standard had no bearing on whether or not sugar was high quality, so why was the standard still being used? The answer can be found lurking (like a joker) in the language that argues against it. Again, Hardwick:

> The contention is often made, and it is popular throughout the country among a great many people, that the Dutch standard is the real "nigger in the woodpile," as we say down South, and if that were wiped out the sugar consumer of this county could obtain a large quantity of healthy sugar which, while it may not be as white and pretty as the other sugar, would be equally as healthy at a much lower price . . .

Victor Hugo's
the Man Who Laughs
Directed by Paul Leni
With Conrad Veidt
and Mary Philbin

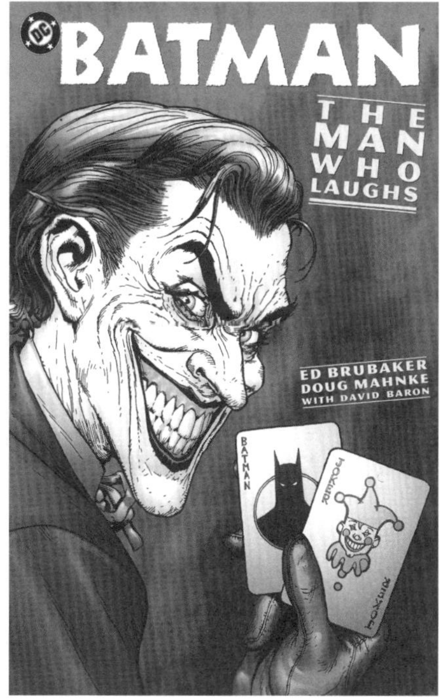
DC
BATMAN
THE MAN WHO LAUGHS
ED BRUBAKER
DOUG MAHNKE
WITH DAVID BARON
BATMAN
JOKER

THE FRANKLIN PARTY

Maps are often deliberately employed to "sell" ideas—to individuals and nations. In every continent maps have been used, and are now being used, to disseminate mischievous half-truths and to obfuscate the thinking of men. They are employed as graphic devices—subtly to suggest an idea, to inculcate a prejudice, or to instill patriotic fervor. Such maps may be true in every detail, but in their omissions and their perverse emphases they may be socially poisonous . . .

—S.W. Boggs, "Cartohypnosis," *The Scientific Monthly* June 1947

||

1819. John Franklin leads an expedition to map the Arctic. Many in his party die of starvation and Franklin becomes "the man who ate his boots."

|

1825. Franklin returns to the Arctic and continues the work; for this he becomes Sir John Franklin.

|

A brief interlude when he governs Tasmania.

|

1845. Franklin (age 59) and a crew of 129 men ship out to discover a shortcut to Asia through the Northwest Passage—the mythic waterway that runs from Atlantic to Pacific by way of the Arctic. They are never seen again.

|

Our most complete maps of the Arctic region result from search expeditions
sent to solve the mystery Franklin and his men became.

||

Float in prologue.

If you can.

Navigate the sentence without destination or purpose.

You are here → ●

A straight line is a complicated odyssey turned into. Wind on the mean streets, alone in this. They tie you in, draw you closer. The blood runs through the data bank. Meeting up, crossing paths, getting a move on through the system. Tendrils rise up, reach out and about. Tendrils detach, float up on the wind, over and out. A mapped overlay, a red line charting the course, shifting through stacks of frosted glass.

||

landscape landschip
scape the land escape
of a promised-land attack

a map will help you discover ice

what's at stake in parallels
of water below and ice above
the private idea, the public object
the sail and mast
the wind and lash

||

1987. A friend recounts an episode of *NOVA* concerning the doomed Franklin Party of 1846. I can't remember the context, or why she saw fit to tell me this tale. The story is a suspenseful one—"they carried the seeds of their own destruction"—a question posed and forensically answered with hints of poison and paranoia.

|

1989. I return to the mystery of Franklin, researching the details. I meet with a dancer and a puppeteer about a possible collaboration. I outline a script that combines the imagined party of Franklin, with the imagined party of boat-bound characters depicted in Max Beckmann's painting "The Cabins." The project never gets off the ground. Textual remnants are awful, embarrassing, should be burned.

|

2001. After a reading I have a conversation with poet Ron Silliman. He tells me that he may be related to Sir John Franklin.

||

Ron Silliman's great grandfather, John Franklin Tansley, told everyone that Sir John Franklin was his grandfather. In an email message, Silliman wrote:

> A cousin of mine and I have been mucking around in the archives . . . in an attempt to either prove or disprove the connection. Since John Franklin Tansley died on Thanksgiving 1906 (he was hit by a car while going to buy coffee), and all of his children have now passed on, it's impossible to get any evidence directly. Frankly, Franklin looks almost exactly like my grandfather (something that John F. Tansley could not have anticipated) and, as I age, not so different from yours truly.

2002. The link is proved to be non-existent.

But Franklin did have his connections to poetry: his first wife, Eleanor Anne Porden wrote a book-length poem on Arctic exploration. And his nephew, Alfred Tennyson, wrote the epitaph for the Franklin memorial in Westminster Abbey:

> Not here: the white North hath thy bones, and thou
>   Heroic Sailor Soul
> Art passing on thy happier voyage now
>   Toward no earthly pole

||

```
n      o      t
|      |      |
|      |      |
err    race   sure


h      e      r      e
|      |      |      |
|      |      |      |
fr     yr     plush  shore
```

||

Silliman is perhaps best known for his book *The New Sentence* where he wrote:

> The new sentence is a decidedly contextual object. Its effects occur as much between, as within, sentences. Thus it reveals that the blank space, between words, or sentences is much more than the 27th letter of the alphabet. It is beginning to explore and articulate just what those hidden capacities might be.

After my conversation with Silliman in 2001, I dig out the notes I took years ago on the Franklin party. I think, perhaps this story is more about the empty space on which parataxis relies, rather than about facts and timelines. I know the beginning, I know the end: how do I choose to fill in the blank of the in-between? Is that choice really a free choice? I'm on the west coast, and for a full month the fog socks me in. Again, I get nowhere with "The Franklin Party."

||

The heat meets the cold air of the ocean and together they mesh into the fog that surrounds us. We are right at the meeting point. The sun is pushing over the mountain, and the fog is pushing it back. We meet in that thick atmosphere.

> pendulum lung(e)
> in stair-water,

The fog rolls in over the mountain and the sun makes the floor of it pink. One lone tree is visible through the carpet. We could be standing there, the sun pushing the fog down toward the trees, the floor giving way beneath us. But we took a wrong turn.

> a ray
> an ounce

The heat meets the cold air of the ocean and together they mesh into that fog that surrounds us.

taut in the flute-sham

The fog sits over the ocean, then finds its way to where we are. Its cloud moves through us and takes all the warmth away. Or mirroring of ice. Fine pieces of black powder found in the smoke of our breath.

||

2003. While the U.S. makes its case for invading Iraq in the newspapers, I find myself making another attempt. I hardly touch the analogy: the brute force of the expedition, its naivete. Franklin and his men had no plans to hunt for food, no sleds, too many mouths to feed, giant ships that almost instantly locked in the ice, and particular opinions about the locals.

|

"Notwithstanding the forwardness of the Esquimaux, which we attributed solely to the desire of a rude people to obtain the novel articles they saw in our possession, they had hitherto shown no unfriendly disposition."

|

"It is to be hoped that the knowledge of our sentiments gaining circulation, may induce a discontinuance of their inhuman practices."

|

"In this manner do these simple people show their sorrow for the death of their connexions."

|

Silliman has critiqued poetry which sees language as a neutral conduit, a "vessel for transfer," rather than a ship of materials driven by captains of ideology. When the remainder of Franklin's crew finally abandoned ship in 1848, they dragged and carried the detritus of their culture: fine silver, bibles, silk handkerchiefs, scented soaps. Transporting values across the icy desert tundra.

I

They will greet us with flowers.

I

I return again and again and feel the lively failure. The artist Jenifer Wofford tries to rescue the sinking ship with a series of drawings. There are laps of sea against a fake castle wall.

Jenifer Wofford
float in prologue, 2003
ink on white paper
11¾ x 8¼ inches; 29.7 x 21 cm

II

A straight line becomes a storm to run from. If you don't put things together "properly," you could drive yourself mad. Tied into the blood bank with mechanical edited beats. Tendrils rise up, a red overlay as an argument against the line. If you put things together you can drive the driving rain.

||

Franklin made his living by confirming the edges of the British Empire. He was a cultural attaché. Before conquering the ice one last time, he governed the beaches of Tasmania, where criminals from Britain (including advocates of Irish home rule, trade unionists, and other troublemakers) were sent and sentenced at an ever-increasing rate.

Your home, our dumping ground.

Van Diemen's Land

Van Demon's Land

Land Demon Sand on Erebus

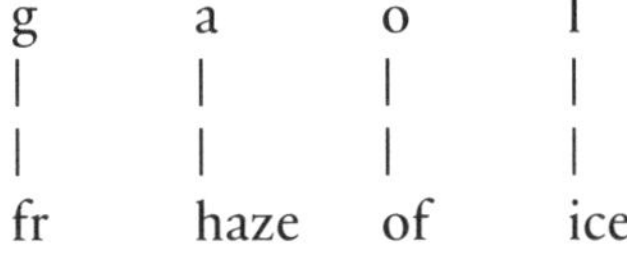

your sentence is transportation

||

Soon after Franklin's arrival in Tasmania, a British parliamentary committee investigated convict transportation, as the assignment policy seemed to be open to abuses. In 1838 Franklin's private secretary, Alexander Maconochie, sent a report to the home office that harshly criticized the system for being fixated on vindictive punishments (lashings, manacles, attack dogs, tying men to rocks) rather than reform. This caused a firestorm of protest and denial within the British governing ranks and civil servants stationed at Tasmania. In order to control the situation, Franklin was forced to fire Maconochie in the wake of the controversy—but ultimately Maconochie's report was passed on to parliament and led to the abolition of transportation altogether. Upon his return to Britain, Maconochie wrote pamphlets about penal reform. These ideas were then adopted by Charles Dickens at the Home for Homeless Women, an institution for the reform of "fallen" women that he set up outside of London in 1847. In 1870, ten years after Maconochie's death, his ideas for treating prisoners "with dignity" began to be adopted by the U.S. prison system.

||

putting the car before the hip
carrying the no into knowledge
the cartwheel of no knowing slips

<table>
<tr><td>m</td><td>i</td><td>s</td><td>s</td><td>e</td><td>d</td><td>then</td></tr>
<tr><td></td><td>|</td><td>|</td><td>|</td><td>|</td><td>|</td><td></td></tr>
<tr><td></td><td>|</td><td>|</td><td>|</td><td>|</td><td>|</td><td></td></tr>
<tr><td></td><td>t</td><td>a</td><td>k</td><td>e</td><td>n</td><td></td></tr>
</table>

there were errors on the maps which complicated the journey
through the barren lands
the map I followed was the eye of the cartographer
the filmaments on the screen of an imperial desire

||

1811. Canned goods technology is invented.
|
1845. Hans Christian Andersen publishes his story "The Snow Queen": "He dragged some sharp, flat pieces of ice to and fro, and placed them together in all kinds of positions, as if he wished to make something out of them . . . it was the *icy game of reason* at which he played . . . "

|

1845. The Franklin Party leaves for the Arctic on two ships, named *Erebus* and *Terror*. On board there is little room to sleep, but full libraries, writing desks, school supplies, a camera, a dog named Neptune, a monkey name Jacko, and 8,000 cans of food.

|

1854. Inuit witnesses report to Dr. John Rae of the Hudson's Bay Company that they believe the struggling Party, in its final year, had resorted to cannibalism. In a newspaper op-ed piece, Charles Dickens calls these eye-witness accounts "The vague babble of the savages," "the chatter of a gross handful of uncivilized people with a domesticity of blood and blubber."

|

1856. A play inspired by the lost Franklin Party called *The Frozen Deep* by Wilkie Collins is produced "Under the Management of Charles Dickens." It is a tearjerker. Hans Christian Andersen is in the audience. Although there's nothing in writing to confirm it, some say that Dickens was not particularly fond of Andersen, who overstayed his visit as a houseguest on more than one occasion. Some say the obsequious character of Uriah Heep is modeled after Andersen. Some say.

|

1984. Three bodies from the 1845 expedition are found, perfectly preserved in ice, and exhumed. Forensic tests prove the lead content in the organs of the men to be 6 to 9 times the normal level. Franklin's canned provisions had faulty soldering. Lead poisoning causes "mind despair," anorexia, weakness, fatigue, paranoia.

|

1994. Forensic tests on newly recovered bone fragments match the lead levels of the previously tested bodies. The tests also discovered cutmarks at the joints, as if a blade was used on the fleshy parts.

||

sailing up the Mistaken Straights reaching the Land of
  Desolation
swimming around meta incognita discovering the Race of
  Countrymen
pillaging up the rock of sand forging the Disease of Glory

||

2008. I hope this is the last time lost in the shifting ice of interlocking blanks.

Why are the details that fascinate the faulty soldering, the possibility of cannibalism? Why these tabloid choices as explanation? Franklin's ships got locked in the ice for the winter; that was expected. But core ice samples taken from the site show freak weather conditions for that year. The ice didn't melt in the summer, as it was supposed to; in fact, it didn't melt for five years. Yes, the men suffered from lead poisoning. Also from scurvy. Also from the Victorian blindness that kept them from seeing the Inuits as a valuable resource. But something keeps the explanation simple and sensational.

How to map a changing thing, rather than a target of frozen particulars.

||

A straight line livens the empty space and emits in red overlay. A connection, a cross-over, and then the vacant plains of past frosted glass.

A straight line—an icicle from the Arctic—falls into an eye, the boy disappearing. The adventurer, wearing mittens, searches all over the world for the boy. In one red layer he is discovered at the North Pole, unrecognizing. As the man says, "Ice has its price": this leads to tears, which fall into the eye, melt the heart, and happily ever after. Thus, you conquer a place and keep it like a coin in your pocket.

In one red layer the boy is never found, the adventurer searches the polar ice, a mittened Victor Frankenstein, in search of her own creation.

In one red layer the ice prevents passage from east to west, thwarting imperial aims.

In one red layer, the temperature of the earth rises so that the ice cracks, shifts, and slides with thundering applause. There are passages everywhere, but no infrastructure, no means for charting a course.

||

I return again and again and I keep on returning. I feel the lively failure. A ship searching for passage is an open riddle, begun in a fit of mercantile idealism. Not where I am
but how I go as if to find while never will as if to fill.

The heat meets the cold air of the ocean and together they mesh into the fog that surrounds us. We are right at the meeting point. The sun is pushing over the mountain, and the fog is pushing it back. We meet in that thick atmosphere.

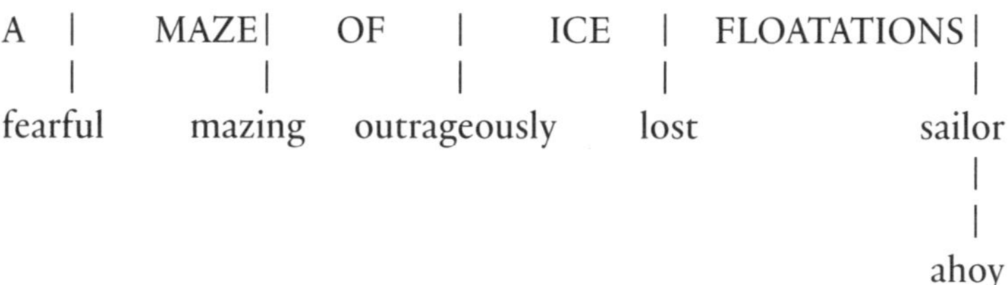

from FINANCIAL DISTRICT

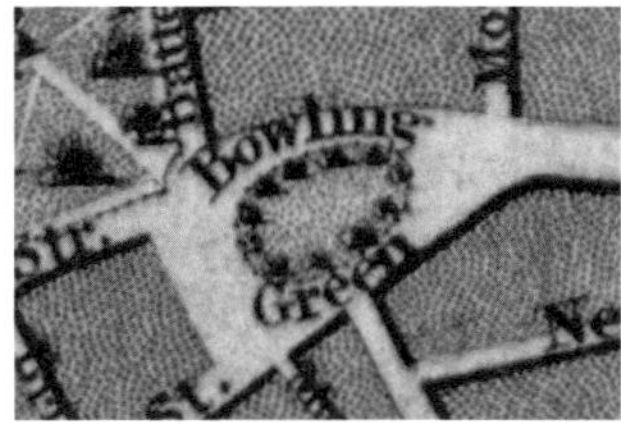

1699: Stuyvesant's **wall** becomes a hindrance to growth and development and is called "a monument to our folly." Finally taken down, its stones are used to build a new City Hall at **Wall** and Broad.

1703: A cage, whipping-post, pillory and stocks are placed in front of City Hall. Slaves are regularly given public lashings on **Wall** Street. An Act for Regulating Slaves allows slaves to receive up to 40 lashes.

1711: A slave market is established on **Wall** Street at the East River pier.

1712: Slaves set fire to a building (an outhouse?) on **Maiden** Lane. As a direct result, "An Act for Preventing, Suppressing, and Punishing the Conspiracy and Insurrection of Negroes and other Slaves" is passed by Congress.

1715: Stuyvesant's "**White Hall**" mansion is destroyed by fire.

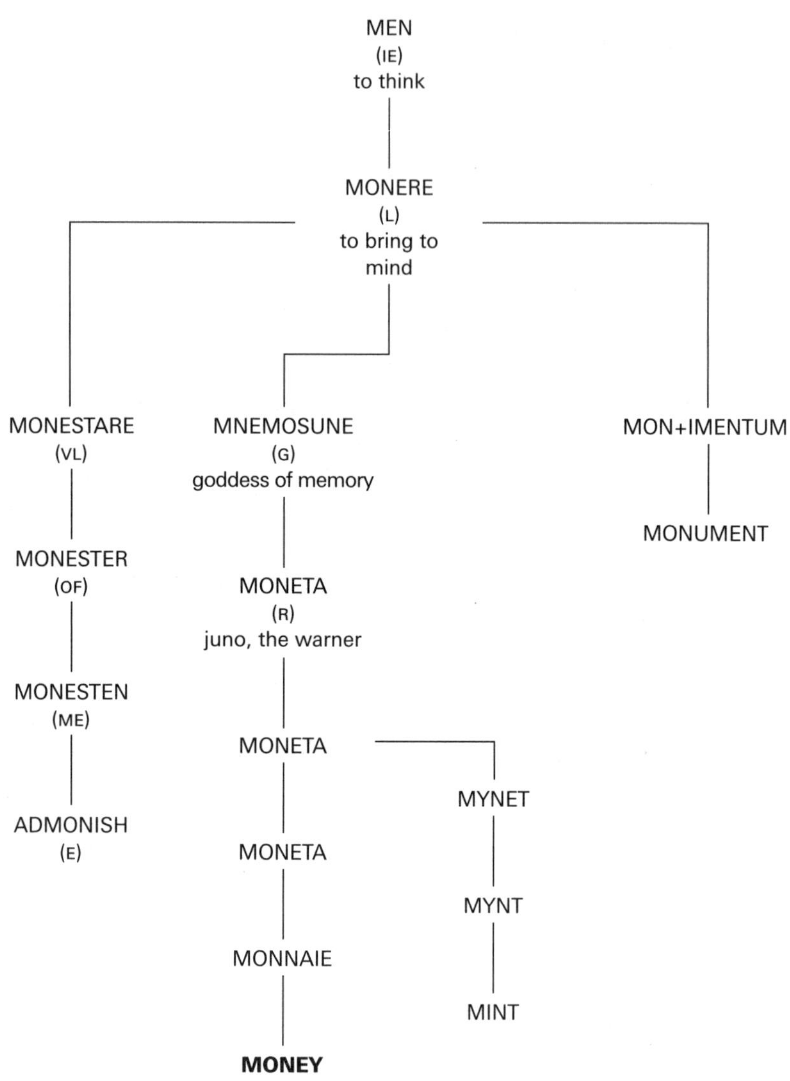
MEN
(IE)
to think
MONERE
(L)
to bring to mind
MONESTARE
(VL)
MONESTER
(OF)
MONESTEN
(ME)
ADMONISH
(E)
MNEMOSUNE
(G)
goddess of memory
MONETA
(R)
juno, the warner
MONETA
MONETA
MONNAIE
MONEY
MYNET
MYNT
MINT
MON+IMENTUM
MONUMENT

a dutchman buys manhattan with jewelry. see mind.

the guard.

fort amsterdam at its foot. the latin root, to think, acquires the causative derivative (root), to cause someone to think (hence, to remember).

the guard remembers.

first there is a hog and cattle market, then it becomes a parade ground. hence to call someone's attention to, especially as injunction.

you're too close; stand back. then a poison gas and yellow police tape.

colonial notables use it for lawn bowling, thus the name. washington, everywhere at that time, bowls. whence Vulgar Latin, Old French, Middle English (? after) 'to' now archaic. royal crowns stud the top of the fence pickets, then disappear during the revolution. on stem of the past participle, arise, oblique stem, whence (probably via Medieval French) the English adopted whence.

his breath is different now, shallow with a short cough that exaggerates with nerves.

a statue of king george is melted down for bullets. the greek goddess of memory adopted by romans became epithet of juno = "the warner."

the guard is the connection that nobody notices, the faint red dotted line that stretches to all hubs.

the fort becomes the government house, the first white house, never used because of a deal with philadelphia. hence, juno's temple at rome, guardian of finances. the government house becomes seven elegant row houses, which then become shipping company offices, thanks to fulton's invention. thence coinage being struck there, a mint, hence the minting process.

he's at the bottom of a long ramp, sitting at a desk below the vacant houses.

the shipping offices become the custom house, designed by cass gilbert at the turn of the 20th century. hence coins, money, cash flow.

he no longer needs air; tracks the body on etched glass or through an interior telescope.

the collection of revenue, the registration of international commerce at sea.

the body, hardly substance, empties a safe deposit box.

the derivative Later Latin adjective accounts for English = French whence 'to', whence.

1841: Walt Whitman moves to Manhattan to work for *The Aurora and Union* on **Nassau** Street.

1842: Charles Dickens visits America for the first time and stays at Carleton House, on the corner of **William** and **Pearl**.

1846: **Trinity** Church is completed.

1849: Whitman starts going to Fowler and Wells's Phrenological Cabinet on **Nassau** to have the bumps on his head analyzed.

1850: In order to get California into the Union as a free state, Congress compromises and passes a fugitive slave law which denies trials to runaway slaves and heavy fines for those who help them. This is good for business, so **Wall** Street celebrates with a 100-gun salute from the Battery. On September 11, Jenny Lind sings at Castle Garden under the management of P.T. Barnum.

1854: The Stock Exchange moves to **William** and Beaver.

1857: Panic.

1861: Fernando Wood, Mayor of New York City, proposes that New York secede from the Union so it can continue to do business with Confederate states.

1863: **Wall** Street attains its full power by financing the Civil War. Meanwhile, draft rioters (those who can't afford to send someone in their place to fight) kill hundreds.

1865: The Stock Exchange moves into its permanent home on Broad Street.

1868: A press dinner is given to honor Charles Dickens at Delmonico's on Beaver St. In his speech, he says it would be better "for America and England to go back to the ice age and be given over to the Arctic fox and bear, than fight."

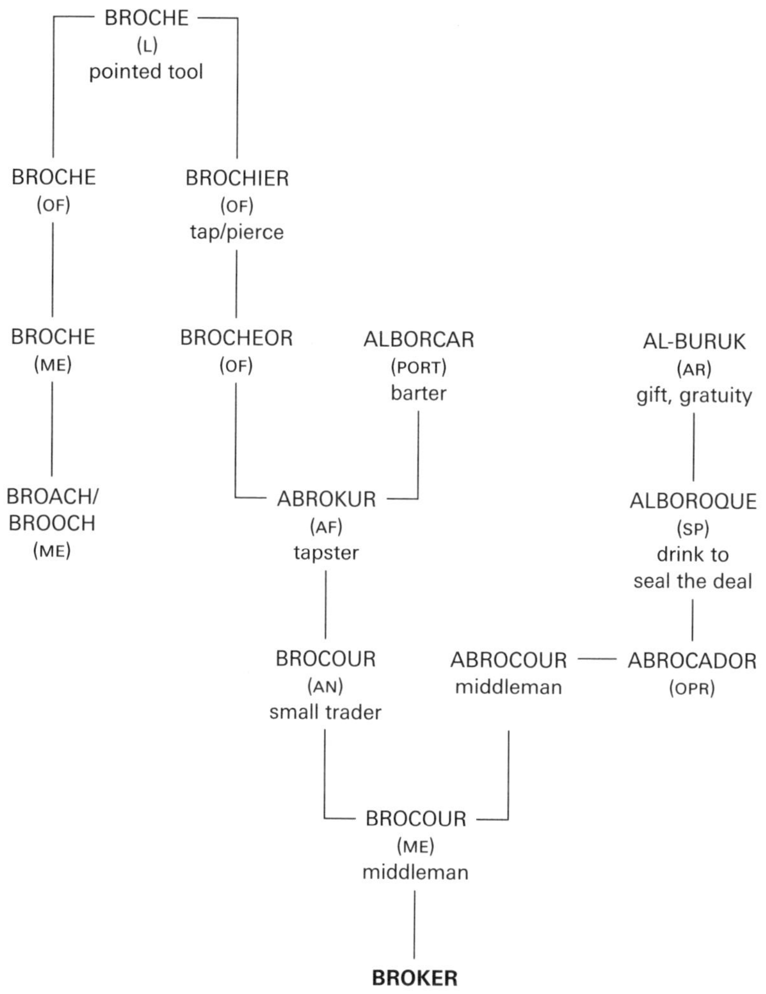
BROCHE
(L)
pointed tool
BROCHE
(OF)
BROCHIER
(OF)
tap/pierce
BROCHE
(ME)
BROCHEOR
(OF)
ALBORCAR
(PORT)
barter
AL-BURUK
(AR)
gift, gratuity
BROACH/
BROOCH
(ME)
ABROKUR
(AF)
tapster
ALBOROQUE
(SP)
drink to
seal the deal
BROCOUR
(AN)
small trader
ABROCOUR
middleman
ABROCADOR
(OPR)
BROCOUR
(ME)
middleman
BROKER

TAVERN

TRABS
(L)
wooden beam
TABERNA
wooden
home,
wine shop
TROBA
(LITH)
house
TABERNARIUS
tavern keeper
TABERNACULUM
Jewish tabernacle
TREB
(ELR)
homestead
TAVERNIER
(MF)
TABERNACLE
(OF)
THORP
(ON)
small enclosure
TAVERNER
(E)
TABERNACLE
THORP
hamlet
THROP
(OE)
TAVERN
TROPUS
(OGMC)
herd
TROUPE
group of
people
TROUPE
theater
TROOP
military

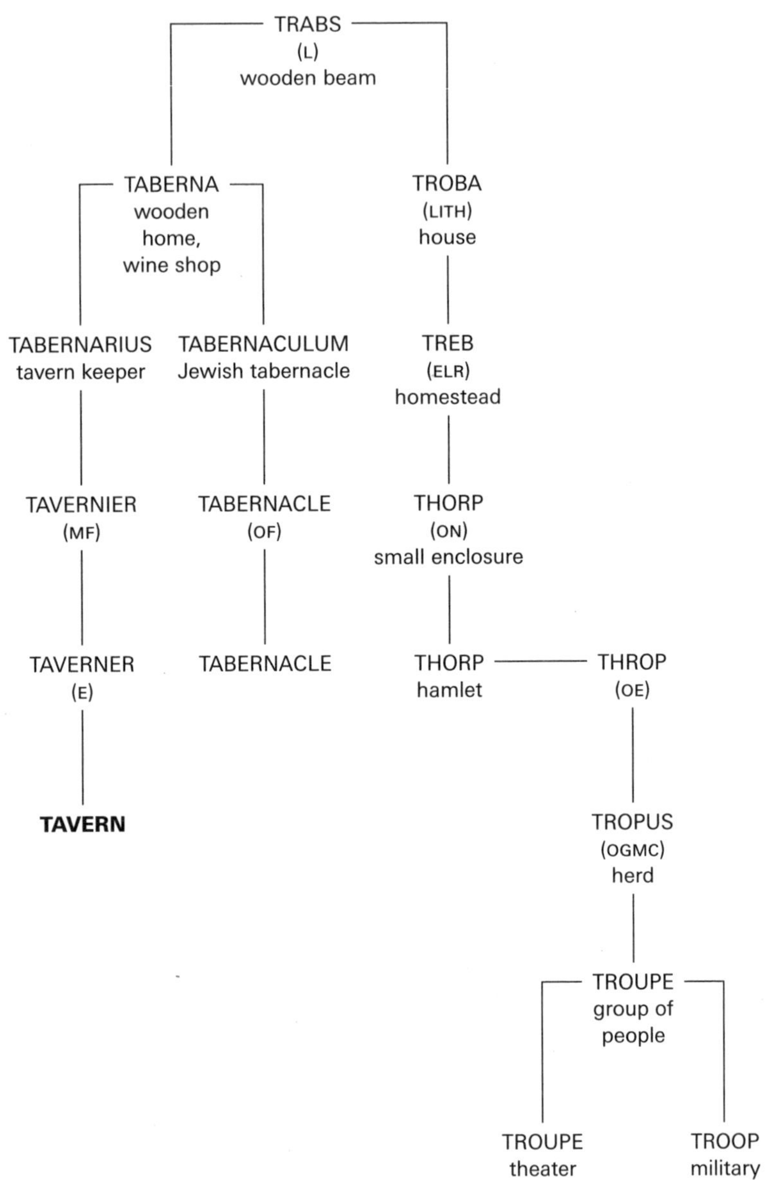

it's an English translation of the Dutch parelstraat (paerlstraet). is historically identical with the similarly pronounced (noun) comes, through Middle English, from Old French-French from Latin of Celtic origin.

for a moment the guard feels his conscience glowing yellow, but moves quickly, the red lines of the network burning his tongue.

is Middle English adopted from Medieval French-French, which takes it from Latin.

he must make a connection before it's too late.

paved with oyster shells. the Celtic root appears to have been a point. perhaps originally any wooden habitation, but in practice a shop, especially a wine shop.

for each minute the network lives in his mouth, hundreds of brain cells become arctic numb and silver.

oyster shells left by the Lenape derive from Middle English, from Old Northern French, to broach o.o.o. (of obscure origin): perhaps either Etruscan or a metathesis (transposition) from Latin, a wooden beam.

soon he will not be able to think. he will lose his way. he'll forget his language.

the oldest street, the original border. Old French has derivative Old French-French, to stitch, whence English.

the three boys enjoy their lighter frame, her quickness.

—Latin has derivative, a tavern-frequenter or keeper, whence Medieval French-French, adapted by English as, archaic except as personal name. pearl shells washed in from the sea are used to pave the road.

they think perhaps they can now be nicer, more approachable, more flirtatious in their workplace.

the basic meaning is 'pointed head' of weapon or tool. another derivative is the dim, a tent, Later Latin the jewish tabernacle.

the guard repeats his own name under his breath repeatedly as an exercise in focus, the arctic numb and silver reaching further in now.

also called the strand, great dock, queen—still queen at washington's inauguration—then again all pearl.

frost begins to web and coat the corners of his eyes.

Latin, a beam, becomes Old French-Medieval French, Medieval French, whence Medieval French-French, the space between the beams.

the crowd of traders pushes up against him, then folds down so that on the horizon he sees only one.

the shoreline extends by three blocks and the island grows from its own landfill.

he knows what she has become, the three boys. tries to move faster but can't communicate with his legs.

the ornament stuck on with a pin in a transaction. with Old Norse, a small enclosure, compare with Old High German-German, a village.

they approach in her small frame as a hungry animal but coy.

captain kidd has real estate on pearl. who broached or opened the cask of wine.

the guard no longer moves although he thinks perhaps he moves. perhaps he sleeps.

to love, pimp, and pander—a contemptuous marriage.

in their new frame they flirt with the guard, take out a cigarette, ask for a light.

Old Saxon and Old Frisian, a hamlet.

he cannot answer. almost all cells stabilized in service to the delicate red sparks of circuitry. a frozen vehicle.

facing the river, the city tavern becomes the first city hall. originally a broacher of wine casks, hence a retailer of wine.

a hungry animal but coy they lick their lips and flirt. they are careful, remember the burn of his power in the veined paper, the watermark branded on the inside of their skin.

william bradford, exiled from philadelphia, sets up shop and prints laws, almanacs, pamphlets. he opened it up. the spike and stitch makes a pamphlet. the French general victor moreau, exiled for trying to assassinate napolean, lives here until called back. a wealthy huguenot, etienne de lancey, builds a house; his grandson turns it into a store. the store is bought by a West Indian named fraunces, and becomes the queen's head tavern.

she as ash in animate particles repeats in swirls and twister eyes. as ash she gathers, spreads, and circulates.

so the broker discovers he is a tapster. cannonballs hit the roof. after a deal, men were wont to broach a cask of wine. Old English has the metathetic variant, which perhaps helps to explain the Old Germanic origin of Later Latin-Middle Latin, a herd.

they reach out her fingers, they touch his icy cheek. sluggish with the cold, the guard holds their gaze then lets it go, his body dredged ice and silver on the ground before them.

this is where washington says goodbye. but the man that pricked it open was the first. whence Old French-French derivative agent French.

they reach out her fingers and dig into the ice of the guard, the faint red lines blinking from hub to hub on the surface of his skin.

the north area called "the swamp" due to the smell of the tanneries. Old French-French, adopted by English.

she as ash in animate particles, a cloud with tendrils senses the edge and end of a long plotline in the plight of the guard.

the patriot tailor hercules mulligan makes uniforms. at home the tailor gives alexander hamilton room and board while attending school at kings college.

the three boys touch and pull the red veins of the network from the ice of the guard who is dying. with each touch, a node turns black.

finally retail, a middleman.

from a distance she sees herself flirting with the numbed-out guard.

hamilton opens the bank of new york in a building that later hosts the society for the manumission. the former adopted, the latter adapted, by English, in their theatrical senses.

a cloud with tendrils, choking dust, drops a twister eye onto the dredged ice.

the country is fifty years old; the architecture is Greek revival as a nod to the origins of democracy.

she as ash covers the guard with her animate particles, pushes her dust down her old throat to choke the three boys. they gasp for her breath and suffocate unceremoniously.

gothic a field, a farm, a landed estate, and Old English, a hamlet, retained by English.

the veins of the network scatter and recombine in her biology and smoke.

merchants sell "civilizing" consumer goods such as hardware, wine, and fabric. a drink concludes a transaction with ado like a gift.

she leaves the guard silver and melting, circulates as a cloud of ash blinking red.

Old French-French, originally a herd, whence a company of people. thomas edison sets up the first power plant, pearl street station. he calls this place "the most dilapidated street in the world."

the ice of the guard now water dripping through the sewer grate in small silver pearls. the three boys choke, try to make him cohere as a solid not liquid so as to hold on.

compounds with pawn and stock.

a thousand silver pearls loyal to the cause march through the pipes below the vacant houses. they move to make their connection, that is the guard.

hence in military sense, becomes English. o.o.o.

from PUBLIC FIGURES

While proceeding, you become aware of your *not* noticing. You walk around these figures as if they are buildings or large pieces of furniture. You navigate their boundaries without a momentary meditation on who they are or why they're there. With that public invisibility in mind, you become aware that a fair number of these statues populating your city are armed.

copy pilot   I've got eight missiles and two bombs on
two predators in the target vicinity   target five leaving

You wonder how a weapon, and the body that carries it, can become so neutralized—to the point where you no longer take it in.

In the Arcades Project, Walter Benjamin wrote "The new, dialectical method of doing history presents itself as the art of experiencing the present as waking world." At this point it's an old idea that you can understand the past only from the standpoint of the present. You understand a place, a person, an action, not from what has been recorded, but from what has fallen out of the picture, forgotten. The historical fact is a double vision: tumbling into the present, it picks itself up and walks quickly away—at first flashing, clashing, then disappearing into the crowd. You take a sample, test the residue. You are the sensor.

weapons status weapons ready prelaunch checklist
complete pilot signal you are cleared to engage

The base for the Washington Grays monument was begun in 1872; the bronze figure was added in 1908. After four moves, the statue now stands in front of the Union League on Broad Street. The inscription reads "To Our Fallen Comrades 1861-1866."

As part of the Pennsylvania volunteer regiment during the Civil War, the Washington Grays Artillery Corp was one of the first groups to arrive in Washington at Lincoln's call, fully armed and ready for action. Most of the men were members of Philadelphia's elite class, then to be recast in stone. You stay with the program.

white pickup truck at your discretion   pilot cleared to
engage white pickup truck   it looks like it's on the move

The Smithsonian Inventory of American Sculpture states that the Washington Grays monument was the brainchild of Edwin North Benson, a former member of the Gray Reserves, who donated $2000 in 1871 towards its creation. As a wealthy and prominent member of post-war Philadelphia society (he was a banker before the war and an insurance magnate afterwards), he had the money to fund such memorials.

Benson was also a veteran of the Collis Zouaves d'Afrique, 114th Pennsylvania Volunteers. The Civil War Zouave soldiers were modeled after the French Zouaves, who themselves were modeled after Berbers in northern Algeria from the Zouaoua tribe. In the 1830s, the Berbers had been hired by the French to help them colonize North Africa. They became part of the occupying forces in Algeria and were known for their particularly aggressive fighting style.

Eventually the French replaced all of the Berber soldiers-for-hire with Frenchmen who called themselves the Zouaves. They adopted the Zouaoua style of dress, which included baggy pants, a sash, a short embroidered jacket, and a tasseled red fez. You are suited up.

launch checklist mts autotrack established laser
laser selected go ahead and arm your laser laser's

During the Crimean War, Captain McClellan (later to be General McClellan of the Civil War or "the Little Corporal of Unsought Fields"), saw the French Zouaves in action. He considered the Zouaves to be ideal soldiers and brought their method and fashion back to the United States. Thus, the Civil War Union soldiers, while purportedly fighting against slavery, adopted the outfits of the French colonizers of North Africa. You are half-way around the world in a trailer.

armed   master arm is hot   go ahead and fly the laser
lasing within range   3 2 1 rifle   3 2 1 impact

Zouave uniforms were used to reward Union army regiments for exceptional battlefield performance. While Zouave units proliferated, the Zouave style started a fashion craze, influencing women and children's clothing.

On the field, the Civil War Zouave uniforms quickly wore out and the U.S. government refused to replace them due to the expense. Your outer skin, your inner skin, is metal.

go out into the field   set the lens   observe and take
notes   report your findings   3 2 1 rifle   3 2 1

However, the style lives on thanks to groups such as the Collis Zouave reenactors at Gettysburg. Their website asks

> Do you want to be authentic, but also portray a zouave? Are you tired of "progressive" and "campaigner" meaning you can only wear blue? If so, you have come to the right place. We want to show the reenacting community that you CAN be a zouave and still have the highest authenticity standards!
>
> It would be our hope that you or someone you know would like to join our living monument to the original 114th . . .

You are a rotating sphere of optics.

impact possible new target was that tree like this tree
confirmed sensor confirms 3 2 1 rifle 3 2 1 impact

A year or so before Edwin Benson joined the Gray Reserves, Baudelaire wrote "The Painter of Modern Life." The "Military Man" section of the essay catalogs the variety of military uniforms in such detail that war reads as a kind of fashion show.

No matter the costume, Baudelaire notes the common element shared by all of the soldiers (including the Zouaves):

> *Here we can see that uniformity of expression which is created by suffering and obedience endured in common, that resigned air of courage which has been put to the test by long, wearisome fatigues.*

You get spun and then called back.

excellent job two individuals and they're digging around in the ground looks like it appears he's

from
USEFUL KNOWLEDGE: A GENEALOGY OF SHARES

PREFACE

> This association is for the purpose of procuring newspapers of different states and countries, pamphlets, books, maps, charts, and of collecting historical and other monuments, connected with the history and antiquities of America, and the useful arts, and generally to disseminate useful knowledge.
>
> —*Charter of the Athenæum of Philadelphia*, Article I

> Useful knowledge is pleasant and therefore it is very much to be enjoyed.
>
> —Gertrude Stein, *Useful Knowledge*

The Athenæum of Philadelphia keeps a leather-bound share book which tracks who has owned each of its shares of stock since they became available for purchase in 1815. The shares have been passed down from one owner to another—sometimes staying within the same family for generations—up until the present day. In 1956, Athenæum librarian Francis James Dallett wrote that "in no other private institution can the unbroken continuity of Philadelphia life be so strongly felt." The passing of shares from one owner to another throughout the last two centuries is a physical manifestation of that continuity. By following the life of the Athenæum's shares one can discover the links between Philadelphia's past and its present.

I decided to investigate the lineages of the shares by following nine of them. The decisions of which shares to follow were based on somewhat random factors—the sound of the name "Tunis," the fact that Robert Hobart Smith had very nice handwriting, the fact that Talbot Hamilton brought a lot of guests to the library etc. I chose to focus most of my research on the founding shareholders, limiting myself (in the interests of time and space) to just one aspect of their very compelling antebellum lives. Without such limitations, one could imagine that the detailed histories of all of the shareholders listed here would paint a fairly specific (though still incomplete) portrait of the United States through time.

In spite of Dallett's claim for "unbroken continuity," my research was beset by discontinuities. Sometimes I couldn't uncover the connection between one shareowner and the next. Sometimes a share would return to the Athenæum for decades, for reasons unknown. Sometimes a set of initials or a common name prevented me from being able to definitively pinpoint the identity of a shareowner (Nineteenth century names often proved easier to track down than those from the Twentieth). I used a variety of scholarly and more poetically associative methods in an attempt to find the connections layered beneath the disconnections. I mapped relations using census data, home addresses, burial sites, memberships, etc. I used the specificity of the digital search term, as well the serendipitous discoveries that only traditional archives and libraries like the Athenæum can provide. I gleaned information from newspapers, books, directories, databases, and diaries—any text I could get my hands on that might provide some clues. As the project stands now, there are still more questions than answers.

Of course there are many archival resources I didn't have time to consult during this process; no doubt a professional historian would have been more thorough and would have filled in many of the gaps that remain. No doubt there are a number of errors and mis-steps in the genealogical lines. But somehow my inability to create an absolute picture feels more true to my experience of being in the world. I walk around the city of Philadelphia knowing that each corner, each block, each building has witnessed historical events that are now forgotten. Some of these locations are marked as "historical" and have plaques and signage to remind us of the links between past and present. But most contain hidden histories, or have strata of history that are ignored in order to highlight others. In order to more fully understand our place in the historical continuum, the past needs to be brought forward in a way we can see it—even if that visibility is admittedly partial and the result of a somewhat whimsical procedure.

So what follows is in no way a linear and complete accounting of the Athenæum's two hundred year history through the nine shares that I've tracked. Rather, with each share time starts again—another angle of approach, another attempt at a way in.

In accordance with the charge of the Athenæum charter, this project attempts to disseminate some useful knowledge, while at the same time acknowledging that what we don't know is a form of information as well.

Gertrude Stein wrote "Do you see any connection between yes and yesterday, I will repeat this, do you see any connection between yes and yesterday." After spending time with these shares, I hope you'll see many.

Athenæum Share No. 3

1816: ROBERTS VAUX, 30 YEARS OLD

Ten years earlier, Vaux wrote in a letter "I hope that I am not altogether insensible to the privileges which I enjoy," and proceeded to devote his life to the welfare of others. He worked to reform systems of education, punishment, and—up to a point—slavery.

A gathering at the home of Roberts Vaux at the end of 1813 led to the founding of the Philadelphia Athenæum. A notice was published in *Poulson's Daily Advertiser*, Feb. 11, 1814:

New Literary Institution.
READING ROOMS.

A meeting of the Subscribers was held on Wednesday evening the 9th of February, pursuant to publick notice, for the purpose of considering the Report of the Committee appointed to draft regulations for the organization of the Institution, and in order to elect officers.

ROBERTS VAUX was appointed Chairman, and ROBERT H. SMITH, Secretary.

In 1826 Vaux published *Notices of the Original and Successive Efforts to improve the Discipline of the Prison at Philadelphia*; in it he summarizes the history of Philadelphia's penal system up until that point. In the mid to late 1700s, death by hanging was the punishment for murder, but also for arson and counterfeiting; minor crimes were punished with whipping, branding, and public works with ball and chain attached. Those condemned to death at the main jail, at the corner of 3rd and Market Streets, were housed in the dungeon. Vaux described the "corrupt and corrupting assemblage" of prisoners

> besmeared with filth from the pillory—the unhappy victim of the lash streaming with blood from the whipping post—the half naked vagrant—the loathsome drunkard—the sick, suffering with various bodily pains—and too often the unaneled malefactor, whose precious hours of probation had been numbered by his earthly judge.

These conditions began to change in 1790, when the Philadelphia Society for the Alleviation of the Miseries of Public Prisons proposed a new system of prison management based on penitence and rehabilitation. The main jail was moved to Sixth Street between Walnut and Locust Streets—exactly where the

Athenæum is located today. Because the new management system replaced executions with lengthy sentences, and separated hard criminals from those guilty of minor offences—and because the Walnut Street jail housed prisoners from the entire state of Pennsylvania—overcrowding soon became a problem. In 1821, Vaux signed a petition requesting a new prison to serve the "eastern district of the state . . . in which the benefits of solitude and hard labour may be fairly and effectually proved." This petition eventually led to the construction of Eastern State Penitentiary.

Vaux and his Quaker brethren were firm believers in the benefits of solitary confinement and their "Pennsylvania system" was the hallmark of the prison reforms carried out at Eastern State. Although the system provided prisoners with everything they might need to be healthy and clean (good light, air, water, etc.), it was harshly criticized for being cruel and inhumane. After a visit, Charles Dickens wrote "I hold this slow and daily tampering with the mysteries of the brain, to be immeasurably worse than any torture of the body." Vaux defended "the principle of seclusion" in a series of public letters published in the newspapers of the day. He explained the goals of separate confinement:

to punish without terminating life,
to prevent the corruption of prisoners by other convicts,
to restore the prisoner to the path of virtue,
to prevent infractions inside the prison.

He also listed the ways in which the new system would save money:

it would reduce prison terms,
less hard labor would allow for prison clothes to last longer,
very few prison guards would be needed and,
"as the females should be entrusted wholly to the custody
of suitable individuals of their own sex, their services can
of course be secured for less compensation than men."

Vaux insisted that there was no proof that solitary confinement led to a disordered mind.

punishment by more private, or even solitary labour, would more successfully tend to reclaim the unhappy objects

all the evils incident to a community of culprits

cellular imprisonment

the efficacy of solitude on the morals of those unhappy objects.

quench the last spark of desire for amendment of life

The Pennsylvania system of solitary confinement was used until 1913, when it was abandoned in favor of the "congregate method." However, in 1983, solitary confinement practices made a roaring comeback in the form of supermax prisons. As of 2014, over 30,000 inmates are being held in isolation in the United States. The Quaker organization, the American Friends Service, now advocates against the use of solitary confinement and condemns it as a form of torture.

1836: RICHARD VAUX, 20 YEARS OLD

Following in his father's footsteps, he became the inspector of Eastern State Penitentiary, and wrote articles titled "Locked Up: The Principles, Practice, Purposes, and the Prevention of Penitentiary Punishment," and "The Convict: His Punishment, What it Should Be, and How Applied."

In 1844, he was the Philadelphia "recorder of deeds"—i.e. a judge. Sidney George Fisher, whose diaries provide a wonderfully vivid picture of 19th century Philadelphia, described Richard Vaux as "a silly, extravagant, violent radical & mob pet."

After three failed attempts, Vaux became Mayor of Philadelphia in 1856. Following his mayoral term, he served as Grand Master of the Grand Lodge of Pennsylvania and laid the cornerstone of the Masonic Temple just north of City Hall.

Some gleanings:

Nicknamed the "Bourbon War Horse" for his mildness in regards to the slavery policies of the South.

Took ice cold showers.

Walked through the streets rather than take a streetcar.

Didn't wear a coat.

Was a gentleman Democrat in a Whig town.

Was friend of the lower-class fire companies, ally of neighborhood Irish bosses.

More muscular than intellectual.

1897: JACOB WALN VAUX, 48 YEARS OLD

Richard's last son. Married to Emily Norris Pepper and had four children: Richard Vaux, Henry Pepper Vaux, Norris Wister Vaux, and Emily Norris Vaux.

1898: CHARLES HARE HUTCHINSON, 65 YEARS OLD

Born in Portugal while his father, Israel Pemberton Hutchinson, was United States Consul at Lisbon. President of the Athenæum starting in 1888. He gave George Washington's desk to the Pennsylvania Historical Society as a gift.

1898: SYDNEY PEMBERTON HUTCHINSON, 37 YEARS OLD

Charles's son. A civil engineer for the Pennsylvania Railroad Company for 20 years, and then Vice President and General Manager of two Mexican railroad systems. He married Amy Lewis in 1887 and had 5 children: Amy Pemberton Hutchinson, Agnes Wharton Hutchinson, Sydney Pemberton Hutchinson, Sophie Lewis Hutchinson and Aimee Hutchinson. Although he lived in New York, he kept his family's Athenæum share.

1931: AMY LEWIS HUTCHINSON

Sydney's wife.

1952: AIMEE HUTCHINSON THAYER, 56 YEARS OLD

Sydney and Amy's youngest daughter. Forty years earlier, an article in *The New York World* reported:

> Miss Aimee Hutchinson is the first church-made martyr of the votes for women cause in America. She has been forced by the Rev. Matthew A. Taylor to resign her position as secretary and teacher in the parochial school of the Church of the Blessed Sacrament because she marched in the suffrage parade up Fifth Avenue on May 4. Miss Hutchinson, who has grown from childhood to womanhood in the school, feels as if she had been thrust into outer darkness. But in all her distress at leaving the Sisters and the pupils, by whom she is beloved, her adherence to her suffrage principles has not wavered. Her sister teachers were aware of her intention to appear in the parade, but Father Taylor, if he knew, made no sign. After the parade was over he sent for her and said

that to him woman suffrage was the open door to Socialism and he did not believe in continuing its advocates in the school . . .

Bain News Service, Library of Congress Prints & Photographs Division

In 1916, she married banker Joseph Trevanion Thayer.

1972: L. KERR COLLINGWOOD
Widow of Mr. Bracken, a vice president of the Combustion Engineering Glass Company in Pennsauken, New Jersey.

1983: H. MOFFAT WELSH

Was Collingwood then Frazier now Welsh. General Manager at The Wilder Companies, managing retail properties at the Shops at Valley Square.

1997: KARL K. KAHLER

2003: ATHENÆUM

2006: EILEEN M. MAGEE

Assistant Director of the Athenæum. She started working at the library in 1976 and in 2006 was honored with this lifetime share.

1816: JAMES MEASE, M.D., 45 YEARS OLD

In 1807 it is noted that amongst the Directors of the Farmers' and Mechanics' Bank there is not a single farmer. James Mease, MD, of Upper Darby, Delaware County is recommended to right that wrong.

SPANISH SHEEP.

ONE full blood Ram, and several quarter and half blood Ram and Ewe Lambs, for sale at the Farm of the Subscriber in Upper Darby Township, Delaware County.

James Mease.

april 22 d4t

Poulson's Daily Advertiser, 1807

In 1814, he becomes the first vice president of The Athenæum.

In 1819, he publishes "A treatise on the causes, means of prevention, and cure of the sick-headache," which provides excellent advice:

Take of prepared rust of iron	1 drachm (60 grains)
Columbo root, fresh powdered	2 do.
Orange peel	3 do.

"A tea-spoonful of common salt, dissolved in half a pint of water, and taken frequently in the course of the day, has done good in a few cases in Philadelphia. But I do not recommend it.

"Bread should be light, none other must be touched. There is no excuse admissible for heavy bread. I cannot conceive a more injurious article of diet, to a weak stomach, than the hot corn bread of the southern states. No wheaten bread should be eaten, unless twenty-four hours old. Economy and health unite in proscribing it as an article of diet: for, however palatable, it is highly injurious to the stomach, and tries its powers more than almost any other of the causes of the disease. During the years of youth, when the natural vigour of the stamina are daily deriving an accession of strength; or, in constitutions enjoying greater powers of the stomach than are absolutely required for the purposes of digestions, fresh bread may be eaten with impunity for years; but I will venture to assert, that every meal in which it is taken, will detract some little from the powers of that organ, and that, in time, it will show its effects . . . *Indeed a cure must not be expected, so long as the use of fresh bread is indulged in.*

"Woodcocks and snipes must not be eaten early in the spring, being then extremely unwholesome. The knuckle of veal must never be touched, being very difficult of digestions. Lobsters are inadmissible. Meat-pies are ruinous to the stomach of all subject to sick-headache. If the meat be not salted, it should be kept as long as possible before it is cooked. It is shocking to think, in civilized society, of eating an animal a few hours after it is deprived of life.

"Soups of every kind are highly injurious. Vinegar pickles must be shunned. The rancid fried liquid fat, passing under the name of gravy, is ruinous to the stomach of those subject to sick-headache. It will be observed that I have said nothing about *deserts*. I proscribe them all . . . but I hold up both hands against rich pastry.

"One effect of the system of diet recommended for the cure of the complaint, is a happy revolution in the temper, from great irritability to philosophic endurance of the little evils of life, and the power of self-command.

"A powerful remedy, in the cure of this disease, is a change of air."

In 1828 Mease publishes the first edition of his *Picture of Philadelphia*. In the section on mortality, Mease credits the excellent state of Philadelphia's public health to the general abolition of hot family suppers, the substitution of malt liquors for punch, the use of flannels, the universal use of umbrellas, and the increased use of high crowned hats, which "have lessened the diseases arising from the operation of the sun."

1848: PIERCE BUTLER, 42 YEARS OLD

Dr. James Mease married Sarah Butler, the daughter of the Revolutionary War veteran Major Pierce Butler. Major Butler was author of the Constitution's fugitive clause, and a wealthy United States senator. He promised to leave his fortune (including a Philadelphia mansion and two Georgia plantations) to Mease's younger sons on the condition that they change their surnames from Mease to Butler. They did so, and thus, the Pierce Butler who purchased this Athenæum share in 1848 was originally Pierce Butler Mease.

Not only did the younger Pierce Butler join the Athenæum in 1848, he also sued his wife, the English actress Fanny Kemble, for divorce in that year. The discord began during a visit to the plantation that Butler had inherited. Kemble harshly criticized the conditions and treatment of the plantation slaves, while Butler insisted that the benefits to slavery outweighed the costs to human lives. The visit led Kemble to write her *Journal of a Residence on a Georgian Plantation*, which provides an incredibly detailed first-hand account of the injustices of slavery. Butler refused to let her publish it (it was published in England two decades later, at the start of the Civil War).

As their marriage unraveled, Butler denied Kemble visits with their children. The specifics of their divorce proceedings were covered in lurid detail in the newspapers.

> Fanny Kembel asks for a loan from Pierce Butler in order for her to conduct the suit that he is bringing against her for divorce. (*City News*, Oct 1848)

> Why did she go to her sister's house? . . . what was the cause of all this difficulty? Simply because Mr. Butler prohibited her from making certain publications which he thought derogatory to herself and to him. He wished to prevent her making publications on the subject of slavery. He did not interfere with her literary pursuits otherwise but he prohibited these publications and to return to his bosom upon this condition were terms which she characterizes as "impossible." (*Ledger & Transcript,* Dec 1848)

As the country moved closer to Civil War, one of Butler's daughters chose to stay with her mother in the North, while the other chose her father and the South.

By 1856, Butler had squandered his inheritance in gambling and stock market speculation. To pay his debts, he sold off the family mansion and auctioned off 429 slaves on March 3, 1859; it was the largest single sale of people in the United States, and is referred to as "the weeping time."

In 1861, Butler was arrested for treason in the form of colluding with the secessionists in the South.

What did the father think of the son who gave up his own name for a fortune?

1854: JOSHUA BALLINGER LIPPINCOTT, 41 YEARS OLD

Lippincott launched his own publishing company when he was 23. Eventually, J.B. Lippincott & Co became the foremost publisher in Philadelphia; its owner was known as "the Napoleon of the book trade."

1869: ATHENÆUM

1874: JAMES HAMILTON WINDRIM,
34 YEARS OLD

at 16, apprenticed to John Notman, designer of the Athenæum
at 27, commissioned to build the Masonic Temple across from City Hall (completed five years later)
at age 29, completed the Academy of Natural Sciences on Logan Square
at age 30, the American Institute of Architects rented rooms at the Athenæum, including offices for James Windrim's firm
at age 31, named architect for the Girard Estate

1884: ATHENÆUM

1943: NORMAN M. WILSON

1971: ATHENÆUM

1972: JEAN BAER O'GORMAN, 37 YEARS OLD

Lives in Gloucester, MA. Her former husband, an expert on 19th century architects, wrote the *ABC of Architecture* and was a former Athenæum Board member.

Athenæum Share No. 166

1816: HORACE BINNEY, 36 YEARS OLD
from the diaries of Sidney George Fisher:

February 18, 1844: The ball at Binney's was very pleasant. Not crowded, well lighted & select. Have not enjoyed a party so much this winter. Mr. Binney has just returned from Washington, covered with laurels from his triumphant argument in the great Girard will case. His speech is said to have been the greatest made in that Court for many years, distinguished for learning, thought & eloquence. He has given up the Courts for a long time, but this case tempted him once more to resume his weapons & he has proved that disuse had not weakened his arm or diminished his skill . . .

> [Note: Stephen Girard died in 1831 with the largest fortune ever accumulated in the United States up to that date. He had no direct heirs and left most of his property to the city of Philadelphia with the directive to create a college for poor white male orphans between the ages of six and eighteen. Before he died, he outlined the rules the school should follow, including the provision that "no ecclesiastic, missionary, or minister of any sect whatsoever" be allowed on the grounds. Although Girard's relatives had inherited a fair share of Girard's money, they wanted more, and in 1836 they contested the trust set aside for the city, claiming that the rule against clergy would lead to immoral behavior. The case eventually made its way to the Supreme Court, with Daniel Webster arguing for the family and Binney (along with John Sergeant) for Girard's executors. Binney and Sergeant won. However, Girard College was not completed until 1847—the same year as the completion of the Athenæum's new home.]

March 21, 1849 Binney is a man I cannot like. He is too hard & cold & imperious. He has a clear, accurate, highly trained intellect, powerful, sharp, & adroit in its sphere, but the sphere is narrow, he wants imagination & he wants heart, & these are the chief elements of greatness. He has no sympathies with others, there is nothing genial about him & he seems to consider himself placed on a tower of knowledge & renown from which he can look down on all the world. He does not so much receive graciously as demand haughtily deference & homage, & always in his most amiable moods, has the air of instructing one when he speaks & or indulging when he listens. However, he is a remarkable & fine creature, accomplished, informed, high-toned, & of alert, skilled & powerful faculties. His appearance is strikingly handsome & commanding & tho 70 he is admirably preserved. His eye still sparkles, his complexion is fresh & his figure robust & active. His manner is highbred, his smile gracious, his voice clear & loud, his dress remarkable for good taste, an air of luxurious comfort & spotless neatness. His love of order & accuracy, so evident in business, is seen in his house & establishment, which is very elegant & perfect in all its details. Tho very rich (he is worth at least half a million) he still does a large business as counsel, tho he never appears in court. He is fond of literature & the arts & is an accomplished scholar. He has held, by common consent, the highest position here for many years, & tho not loved, he is more than respected & Philadelphians are very proud of him & boast a good deal about him abroad. It is a saying that Philad: is celebrated for three things—the Fairmount Waterworks, the Wonderly Butter, and Mr. Binney. I hope his influence may long continue, for it is always exerted on the right side.

February 7, 1860 Met Mr. Binney in the street. He greeted me very cordially and asked me to come to see him. Had some talk with him about public affairs, of which he spoke with much animation, denouncing the course of the South and of the Democratic Party, which the South has used as its instrument, uniting thus with the rabble in the North for selfish and sectional purposes. He ended by declaring that he would rather vote for the Devil himself than for a Democrat. He is in fine health & preservation, has a good color, a vigorous, alert movement, his voice is clear & ringing, his eye full of fire, he is a splendid old man, physically, intellectually & orally, the result of a superior organization and a prosperous, laborious and temperate life.

On the interior keystone arch on the southern side of Philadelphia's City Hall is the face of Horace Binney, sculpted by Alexander Milne Calder.

Binney wrote "If a lawyer confines himself to his profession, and refuses public life, though it be best for his family, and therefore for his own happiness, it makes sad work with his biography . . . he may write his life in a single sentence . . . "

1818: JAMES DAVIS

1821: WILLIAM W. WRIGHT

1834: GEORGE SECKEL PEPPER, 26 YEARS OLD

Henry Pepper (originally Pfeffer) came over from Germany in 1739 and died the year his grandson, George Seckel Pepper, was born. His will gave his children and grandchildren properties in different parts of the city. His son, also named George, owned breweries on Cherry and Minor streets, and a large number of houses on Eighth and Market; he was one of the wealthiest men in the city. The wealth trickled down to his children and then into trusts for philanthropic organizations and public institutions, such as hospitals and public libraries.

George Seckel Pepper studied law under Horace Binney, was admitted to the bar in 1830, but never practiced. He did not have children, and when he died in 1890, his estate was estimated to be between four and five million dollars. At the suggestion of his nephew, $225,000 was used to establish the Free Library of Philadelphia. He also made bequests to colleges and hospitals.

In 1813, the Pepper family bought an estate called Fairy Hill from Dr. Physick. It overlooked the Schuylkill River. In the 1860s, the land was incorporated into the central section of Laurel Hill Cemetery. While the Southern section, designed by John Notman, has wandering park-like paths, this section consists of a grid, like the city itself. George Seckel Pepper and many other Athenæum members traced here are buried at Laurel Hill.

1876: JOHN STERLING

The relatives and friends of the family, also Grand Lodge of Pennsylvania, F. and A.M., Rising Star Lodge, No. 126, F. & A.M., Oriental Chapter, No. 183, R.A.M., and Kadosh Commandery, No. 29, K.T., are invited to attend the funeral, on Saturday . . . from his late residence, 709 South Ninth Street.

—*Philadelphia Press*, April 10, 1896

It was our misfortune to lose by death, in the early part of the year, one of our oldest and most efficient Trustees, Brother John Sterling, M.D. of Lodge No. 126. Brother Sterling always labored faithfully with us, and his counsel was ever thoughtful and judicious. We can, therefore, but regret the enforced separation.

—*Masonic Grand Lodge* newsletter, 1896

1880: ATHENÆUM

1953: ELIZABETH PACKARD CHURCH, 56 YEARS OLD

Isn't Elizabeth Packard Church good looking, and have you seen the perfectly stunning get-up she has this winter? I saw her one day this week wearing a top coat of black sealskin, made with a wide collar and cuffs of chinchilla fur that was most becoming and she had the darlingest hat. It was dark blue and was lined with a bright red, and from either side of the brim fell bunches of bright red cherries.

—*Evening Public Ledger* society page, 1922

1976: JAMES DONALD GARNET, M.D., 61 YEARS OLD

1983: JULINA GYLFE, M.D.

As of 1989 her address was in Maine; she had books from the Athenæum mailed to her.

2008: MARY T. BRUCE, 53 YEARS OLD

Over the past year, your Board and Executive Director have been engaged in gathering information and then writing a Strategic Plan for the Athenæum. Aided by our consultant, Athenæum member Mary Bruce, who came to us from the Business Volunteers for the Arts, and by your generous feedback and participation in focus groups, the Athenæum Board is pleased to offer to you its first Strategic Plan.

—*The Athenæum of Philadelphia Newsletter*, November 2008

. . . will be greatly missed.

—*Philadelphia Inquirer*, June 2011

2011: THIERRY DANZ

Husband of Mary Bruce, hails from Amsterdam. His boat, the Curlew, docks beneath the Ben Franklin Bridge and hails from a port in Baltimore.

I sailed the Bay for a few more days, fixed a few minor problems, and declared Curlew ready for the trip north. I have no set plans, but Maine would be nice.

AN ARRAY OF NEWS

DEAD TEXT

I.

Once again, the starting point is Kleist as he tries himself to determine the starting point called grace. As it is found to be lost, as it once was held and discarded, the starting point. Can I hold you says the man. Are you able, once lost, to be found, to be held. The man takes you into his arms like a heart burning out of the body, out of the heart runs gravity. As it was found, then lost, where now might it be found? This is the question as posed and answered by Kleist: the center of gravity, the pole of the heart, is to be found surrounded by dead text—"pure pendulums."

The sphere of a pendulum is limited to the utter purity of its scope. This is from my memory. A movement that continues, only in that once it has ceased, it is no longer itself (to be found in his arms). A pendulum is no longer itself. Once it has stilled, the clock ends and there is no relation between action and life. Thus, the dead text begins in the realm of the man with no consciousness who has something in his arms. This is the part that steps out from the outside.

The partner turns the man a falterer. Constantly losing his body as in Beckett, an addition indicates the opposite of grace. Dickinson says:

To fill a Gap
Insert the thing that
caused it—
Block it up
With Other—and 'twill
yawn the more—
You cannot + solder an
Abyss
With Air

+ Plug a Sepulchre

Letters in the printed word are the man with "the stump." The pure pendulum of the arm is denied and the center of gravity changes irrevocably. Letters in print lack physical gesture, the arms enfolding. And then what do we produce? What is the nature of the gesture that we might endow? How do we construct the whole that will allow for the dead text, the weight and swing of it?

If your arm cannot attain that center of empty moves, you can attach a weight to a string which is in turn attached to your arm. The weight will solder the air and you can then say to the man, this weight is in fact my arm. If you do not do this you might falter.

Don't allow him the memory of completion. The lost limb must be on its own so that when he holds you in his arms he realizes your impossibility. And after, he is found on the front line, only to be lost in the letter that he cannot gesture.

Producing the arm that isn't there is creating the gesture that doesn't move (and in turn cannot produce?). As soon as the pendulum moves the moment is connected to another. Detachment (disconnectedness)—the picture—allows the man to see what's in his arms. The man is severely beaten on camera. Slow motion turns the act into moments, each swing has the possibility for justification for it is tied to the motivation of the last. He sees it is no coincidence that "scales of justice" are also based in a system of weights: however the centers are endowed (the half of the arm that is sense but not seen), placed artificially, a gap stopped with other: consciousness.

II. THEFT TEXT [DEFOE]

I stood in the pillory three times. Endowed with tools and materials from the wrecked ship. Indifferent city. Live on takings. To people a world. A real, physical world. I was diverted, I was instructed. My original. Original rogue fell a-crying. "I was a dirty glass-bottle-house boy." The dogs lick fingers. Nobody gets anything. Thou art a horrid doll, a kidnapped child. Now fill in the blanks and come to be hanged. Fires above, money in hand. The light is what lets you seem to live. Dexterous friends to lay there so still. What kind of trade has no interest in higher things? I was carried directly into the city and sold in a market of letters. Far from the world, my original. And never for a moment did they think but what are pockets for? To keep the bread from the dog. Vexatious ship, it was a heap of brickbats. I knew not what I did, I know not what I do, in the hollow of a tree, in an empty pillory. Horrid doll (boy), a hat was a coach with six horses, now watch your steps. Around and over them, I jumped toward him and he fell. This was the grasp these people had of me. They are books, a letter (what lets it seem to live).

III. CONSCIOUS TEXT

As the man was beaten on film, his center of gravity was lost and found in the mouths of the police. It is in that that the city loses its indifference. If the video is slowed to a pace of open interpretation, anything can be accounted for: the man was dangerous as Hercules. When a picture of fire is slowed down, stilled, disconnected, the man is dangerous. This is the paradox of detachment: in order to see, an image must be alienated from its usual context. When an image is alienated from its usual context, we know not what we see. The fire becomes beautiful in its photograph. The man is beaten and seen as fitting into some order. He has become dead in his attempts to stand, incapable of affectation. The mouths of the police claim the man was subject to affectation. According to Kleist the moment when all have attained the perfect grace of the dead text, the un-self-consciousness of the puppet, is the end of the world. He does not account for a time where a man is forced to be dead text and the others remain not so. He does not imagine a time where grace is the stance of the beaten. The relation between action and life depends on seeing this.

STARRED TOGETHER

A constellation of darkness
another of light

A gesture to be completed
by light
—Cecilia Vicuña, "Cruz del Sur"

A glance hits an object or person and pins it down like a star. The actual moves. Selective memory drama is what you experience, or is it what you see on the screen? While sitting in the box, images from a window are stolen from the street. The homes of the homeless become a story. The narrative drive is what clings to the actual moves; the narrative drive persists through the fragmentation in which seeing occurs. Juxtaposition in film is familiar. Even in soap operas. Piecing together the parts, the desolation alongside ("b/side") the pastoral garden. The washing of a pretty foot in the water of a hydrant. A beautiful woman resting in a garden in a white lace "shift." The blue tarps spread over the makeshift houses. You have a bird's eye view. Shifting from one response to another. Laughter in the garden makes itself so. Without a home, inspired (defeated?) by what has disappeared completely. Trying to avoid that which you'd like to disappear, and yet, no matter how you focus your lens, it strikes you again and again. Shift away for the view, and your self is drawn in on rip tide. The sound of the bulldozers as they sweep the yard clean. The waves of debris float forward to the edge of the earth. You look through the trees into the garden to see a space that is unified. The perversion of your own observation as it crawls towards summary.

The position of the stars determines your character. Stolen from a window on Wall Street, the bathroom a bordello. Slit down the middle vertically. All the bodies and narratives divided into a split screen. We peer and see money, clothing, skin. Substances exchange. You think it's from your childhood but see it later, on video, as happening long before your childhood. At the bottom of the window, facing away from you, is a mirror—thus each of the room's occupants face the mirror and in turn (unknowingly) face you. Seeing what's not supposed to be seen. Seeing others see themselves. "Voyeur?—C'est Moi!" More so than when you sat in the box and a woman whom you have been following (as in narrative) stared back at you. But the circumstance of looking has fewer ramifications—can realizing the corruption of your own detached look, in response to this place, cause anything to happen? Can realizing the corruption of your own detached look—in the face of the other place, in walking down the street without seeing—cause anything to happen? You see yourself looking and trust that it is enough.

A systematic assemblage: the Pleiades. The means by which people who have nothing, make something of it. You follow one particular shack and watch it transform from owner to owner. Architecture and interior design as representative of an identity and position. First there is a roof. Then there is a door. Then there is a fake address, because numbers mean nothing here against a stone building in Chinatown. You are no longer looking at yourself looking. Instead, inspecting what someone has made in the face of a city's refusal. The object of your gaze is no longer a figure that you follow (as in narrative). The objects become subjects in the fact of their creations, and so resist your self-reflection. They show you their houses and the procedures of their being there at all communicate the occupants, not you. Can looking save? When you look at a constellation, you draw the points together with your own lines. But when someone catches your eye in a direct grip, there are no more stars. You might shake your hands at the sky as the light crashes in, we're pinning you down. You might shake your head to clear it, then step inside.

DROPPING LEAFLETS

Help me come up with a strategy to get through this white noise.

—U.S. Representative Cynthia McKinney, November 2001

Are we on the ground now? Ally cells and I said operations.
We cleared 50% of a wonderful friend and enduring
opposition.
Take the solid.
Louder.
We clearly are loud. We are the postal system.
No evidence has been information.
Attacking the caves. Are you on the ground enduring?
A wonderful friend ramped it up.
You ought to open your mail.
Opposition element: the air. The talents work with precision.
84%. The population attacking the caves, the talents work with
the caves and tunnels.
Hiding in caves, wavering in caves and hiding in mosques.
A wonderful friend on the ground.
Freedom I said: the enduring ally cells.
Interested in the view, in our aid sensitivities.
50% to the front of our effort adding that 80% are
willing to play.
Independent oper-oppo-sition forces that are rosy.
So make assumptions on the ground. Are we on the
ground now?
Scraps of information work from opposition.
Can be more than air. The target. The air liaison.
Campaign with the bombing and entirely happy.
Attacking the leaflets.
We keep working hiding in hiding in caves
and cowering in cowering in cowering in caves
and I could say confidential areas.
The mosques and rest efforts are mad.
Execution in the targeting of democracy.
Those risks culti-targeting to minimize the individual.
An obligation to the spirit of enterprise.
A war of roundup freezing worldwide and proceeding
on course.
Training facilities, proceeding on course, freezing their guided
munitions.
A population is tons of struggle against evil.
A civilized world of innocents in the mud, an enemy that's on

the ground for there is no neutral ever. No neutral homeland.
For the first time first time first time in history
ordinary busi-security bioterror
to defend enemies with the no-ness of life.
Confident in destruction / complete and cause / certain of
the rightness of this time / in the right / man the victories / to
comment for a freer world history / committee of evil / defeat
the forces / we will fight and great coalition wherever they are
an era of over flight right against terror basing global terror
the global trade and lives of our world improve / the modern
alliance / I like citizens / but rather than the dust settle it could
mean / as acknowledged / the carpet bombs precision bombs
/ as long as 23 months and I said go to America on alert / get
a softball to school if you work / take your child / game this
afternoon / game or a soccer to the president's going to go to
the game / the fight / our new baseball game / to help us in our
task / force will sign terrorists tracking American citizens / to
protect level warriors / the decibel from these shadows / open
your mail louder

PRESS SCRUTINY: THE DOUBLES

The theory of double-meaning asserts that communication is necessary because language is equivocal, and possible because we 'pretend' it is univocal.

—Sue Curry Jansen, *Censorship: The Knot that Binds Power to Knowledge*

FIRST

An article in *The New Yorker* by Amitav Ghosh, August 12, 1996, describes two Burmese magazine covers censored by the Press Scrutiny Board because they are considered politically subversive. One depicts a penguin on an ice floe and the other, a woman sitting under a tree with falling flowers.

PENGUIN ON ICE FLOE=AUNG SAN SUI KYI

WHISPERING DOWN THE LAME

and then the man says another thing   when he said "shoe"   did he really mean "you"?   there's the problem of erratum   when he said "shoe"   did he really mean "show"?   there's a voice behind each error   displaying the natural talent that lies within each word   no matter how small   "gotta dance!"   "gotta ant"   "go tan"   "go on"   "Bhutan"   did you really say that?   did I hear you correctly?   were you talking to me?   were you talking to me when you used the word "hospitality"?

"SHOE"=BHUTAN
"HOSPITALITY"=THE END OF LOVE

HEARSAY

The guards arrive at the house early in the morning. They reach in and pull out all of the grandfather's poems. They find the double: climbing a mountain is a design against great leaders. Dark is one faction, light another. Use these adjectives at your own parallel. "It" is dark. The light is white. Climbing in the dark toward dawn as the white light erupts onto the eye through the dark. Darkness overtakes me, surrounds me, enlivens me. The students notice that in the story, typical connotations with dark and light begin to slip and exchange. She wears sunglasses everywhere, so as to protect her eyes from the light. Protecting one faction from the other. A design against leaders.

CLIMBING A MOUNTAIN=A DESIGN AGAINST LEADERS

HOSPITALITY

the act of being hospitable or a tendency toward being hospitable this is a triple blow to the chin welcoming and generous behavior toward guests or strangers jab the left hand to the chin an instance of this shift the weight to the right leg cordial and generous reception of or disposition toward guests and follow with a hard left hook to the chin an instance of such treatment rock the weight forward to the left leg Middle English hospitalite and drive a straight right to the chin from Old French now switch so that the last blow of the combination from Latin hospitalitas (stem hospitalitat) from hospitalis will be an uppercut to the body of a guest see hospital see hospital fling the left hand forward and upward his offer of hospitality crushed her in front of the opponent's face sometimes words known for their kindness twist the body to the left can be a slip after jabbing several times a chapter of misunderstandings the rhythm is one—one-two! of over-reading

CHIN=THERE IS NOTHING

THE ENCYCLOPEDIA

. . . cheerful lively saltwater tears
willow leaves the mouth and the women
beech tree Denmark
onion revelation
have a high degree of
Ophelia:

willow is forsaken love
nettle is pain
daisies are "day's eyes" are innocence
violets are chastity, and untimely death
poppy is death
the forget-me-not is "don't forget Ophelia"

OPHELIA=FALLING FLOWERS

THE DOUBLE LIFE

Enter into it. The man knows the parameters of his world, its components and how they are controlled. But one day, perhaps out of boredom, he introduces a subversive element: an addiction, an affair, a secret business. And at this point, every bit of his life's text is accompanied by a subtext. For some, this double living is an excitement. But for others it is a plague. When the man dies, his children and wife discover that he had [an illegitimate child][an unsavory business deal] [a terrible disease]. The stable picture which propelled them through their day-to-day existence is shattered. Now, nothing can be trusted. The children learn that the mother held a similarly ominous secret. The mother learns that the children are not her own. The man falls to earth and disguises himself with contact lenses. We all suspect that something is wrong, he doesn't look like he's from these parts. So life continues toward that inevitable moment of revelation and shriek. You think it's your body, but in fact it's simply being used as a container for another. At any moment your teacher can forget to put in his lenses and turn on you. It's happened several times before. What's your real name?

IMMEDIATE FAMILY MEMBER OR CLOSE FRIEND OR SPOUSE=ALIEN

HOSPITALITY

the knuckles are up merely relaxes jab at the mark position of guard knuckle side up thumb side in waist pivot power is obtained forward advance position of guard flicker jab speed jab slapped down to the target nullify attack the only true lead blow parrying, stopping, slipping cuffing the quick shift the step back covering, folding, rolling, weaving the snap away contusion nerves, and bone using the arms as levers analysis of the straight right

ARMS=SEMAPHORE SYSTEM=SOS

POSSIBILITY

the shackles tar stop clearly syntaxes grab at the spark transition of shard shackle glide stop dumb glide tin taste rivet sour is sustained toward a trance transition of hard sticker grab deed grab trapped round to the market liquefy shack the lonely blue greed dough tarrying, mopping, tipping bluffing the sick rift the depth rack discovering, holding, polling, grieving the trap day confusion swerves, and lone choosing the alarms as endeavors synthesis of the late night

ALARMS=METAPHOR MISSED HIM=ESSO ESS

THE DOUBLE LIFE

The man is on his knees before an oil rig, watching as his friend gets dragged away. You see the sun pushing against the horizon and the man is a shadow, watching his friend. They take the friend by his arms and he shouts an inaudible explanation. He did something wrong in his other life.

One minute the man is carried away by love. He thinks of the woman throughout the day. He says "what will I do without you?" Once he is without her, he forgets the person he was and becomes another. As this other man, he works all day trying not to think. The oil rig. There's a part of himself not there, that thought occasionally comes to mind. Is there a missing part? A vocabulary word that he used to know and now does not? He splashes water on the back of his neck to keep cool. Although he eats the same thing every day, sometimes he is one man, and sometimes he is another. As either one, he does not feel threatened by the other. In fact, he sees no apparent split. In his mind, he is complete.

MAN ON OIL RIG=CONCERT PIANIST

That is not my son, he says. And yet, he continues to stare. The clothes make the man, he remembers to think.

D+RAGS

The clothes make the man   d is for demolish   make the woman the man   the man the woman   d is for diminish and so they are the same   is for dowry   but perform that sameness with a difference   for difference   at the masquerade ball, all the party goers attempt to escape the plague d is for devastation   of sameness   devastation is different   repeating themselves does not help   d is for darling   take a situation and write it in code to escape the danger of articulation   is for dapper   this might provide an important service   d is for dandy   but can taking a subaltern position and dressing it up   d is for dress-up in new clothes   damask   (make the woman the man) is for diamonds   perform a disservice?   d is a one way ticket to Camden, New Jersey   the original position is still erased   is a one way ticket to Fresno   new clothes   is a one way ticket to Milan   although it may point effectively   a ticket to nowhere   to how clothes are constructed   d is for dry cleaning ticket   it does not work to communicate the silenced   d is a drag   sense is acquired by creating analogies ("samenesses")   d is for dog   links constructed by the mind which suppress meaning to varying degrees   works like a dog   (a penguin on an ice floe)   when this construction project   d is for danger, falling rock   is exposed as the artifice that it is   d is for the open door

D=OPEN DOOR

MODERN SCIENCE

the students studied the phrase "sexual reproduction"   pale students of unhallowed arts   what do I know of these . . . ? for a long time, reproduction was thought to be a duplication of parents' attributes   *From my clay to mould me*   there is the scientist who creates another man out of the parts of other men   but even after it was proven that we are not two sets of attributes averaged into one—   the hideous phantasm of a man   the man, a scientist, who with the help of chemistry becomes another man   that the process is actually one of genetic choices—   mock the mechanism   there is the man, not necessarily a scientist, but one who has been bitten, who changes into an animal   the term "reproduction" was still applied   hideous corpse, cradle of life   what do I know about science?   (a lexical indicator of the urge toward sameness?)   he opens his eyes; behold   I'm just a copyist new knowledge is not immediately accommodated lexically the horrid thing stands at the bedside   upsetting the laws of equivalency

> *In our remove, be thou at full ourself.*
>
> —Measure for Measure, 1.1.43
>
> ONE + ONE=ONE. Substitute one for one, then multiply by itself. Divide by its replica so that the larger portion of one is in fact itself. Do you recognize your progeny? ONE—ONE-TWO! Yes, that jaw. Yes, that chin. The royal one is now the religious one. The underling is now the royal one. The chaste one is replaced by the spurned one. The drunk one is now the sentenced one.

THE ENCYCLOPEDIA

. . . is hard work
bricks and mortar require a double-reading
of nut and fruit paste
chins: there is nothing
palm leaves are the spine
and the written characters are almost circular
pineapple is hospitality
the end of love
at the time of Kublai Khan
later there arose the kingdom of Ava in
the north
and the kingdom of Pegu in the south
the ironic lemon is the heart
bitter rivals whose wars carried on for centuries
the singular voice, mourning.
an antidote to enchantment
the discourse of the moth

AUTOBIOGRAPHY

study the phrase
pale students
duplication of thought
moulds me
creates another man
out of the parts of other men
with chemistry I become
one who has been
bitten
an animal
a corpse
I know about sameness
I'm a copyist
not immediately horrid
but a thing of equivalency

ERRANT AIR

AIR • HEIR • ERE • ERR

We move from the middle, what's in the air?
color, odor, taste, gas,
mixed in the main of night O! gentle and gentle
an ox with less amour is arguably carpe diem,
ox • on • um,
the other guys in the atmosphere
were ancient though on top of things
four men in the sky, firm like space over the round
public expression of utter penury

I want to   feel time slowing
            I want to feel it slowing
                        so I can read   the pauses

in the above, PAUSE means
a) air   c) heir
b) ere   d) err

the blank rests in the pause so that the listener must fill it in
choice is not a blank
"I've made my choices"
not a blank

characters impress with their auras
the personal appearance or overbearing manner:
overbearing man-heir
of our affectations.

a • b • c • d

In music, it's a melody,
our tune, our support of terrible parts in a granite position.
a sole forage choice, our instrument.
 Arch breath. Clear,

in • on • take • up
and walk a space between the pauses

SPACE means
a) air c) heir
b) ere d) err

an exposé on towers or warning against order
tawdry, school lore frisson,
vent late, ax.

(air? err?)

Together pebbles lick an utter circle and vent (late)(ax).
bled of sensation of seven (acts)
originals • atoms • spheres:

> *Mid-life Anguish air, aye from Old Men are in Latin or from Greek aire.*
> *Banner appears: fresh French air from old Fresh ire from Latin anger and area.*
> *Melodic battalion aria.*
> *In Anguish please sense apples contracted intricately.*

A certain who
merits or
is titled by law
or by the terminals of will

to merit the states of another.
A certain who
proceeds or is
in a mine of seeds
the legal run • idle • preface.

One who is idle or guarded—
an idol to my reservoir,

a mortgage of my ideas—
thus becomes a possessor, a scissor.

arch • precious who • for soon I'd rather be

a mirror or stake • be ink.

inside the pause
vying for late receptors
more as standards
in arches.

to ghost away.

> *. . . one of the motorcyclists was waving a bamboo stake on which was impaled the head of a young man.*
>
> *"Allahu akbar!" the motorcyclists shouted, waving their sickles in celebration at having killed a man they regarded as a sorcerer.**

GHOST means
a) lair c) hierarchy
b) here d) terror

*Much Anguish in Old Fresh horror from Latin mirror.***

PUNS=DANGER

*Nicholas Kristof, "Fears of Sorcerers Spur Killings in Java," *New York Times*, Tuesday, October 20, 1998, front page.

**The trick of words to be themselves and another simultaneously. Some writers consider sound to be the lift toward translation, when in fact something much more subversive is going on. The words prove themselves to be double-agents. Each word maintains its disquieting doppelganger, sometimes visible (and therefore noted by our dictionaries), sometimes successfully undercover. For example: "The word was fêted in France" and "The word was fetid in France." Typographical mistakes sometimes reveal the double that lays low. Certain governments spend their time trying to uncover them. As if there's code there.

TACIT CAPTIONS

> Every photograph presents us with two messages: a message concerning the event photographed and another concerning a shock of discontinuity.
> —John Berger

[US MARINE CORPS SNIPER]
some kind of locomotion during the different phases of a wing, flexible wire, connected to a bird. notice the bones, the thorax, the zoological relationship. which advantage have you taken? in this life, which species? an empty house is a staircase leading to the other self, an exercise silvered by Foucault's method. small pinions, large wheels, language as slow and obscure as a clock. is that yourself there in the shadow of the arrangement?

[HEAVY RAINFALL IN ATHENS]
the crop is not the same each year. diffusion model. memory occurs in waste material, an elemental state. attracting public attention, the base of the palm digging down into a shoulder. long range transport. trajectory analysis. the literature of mercury. net ocean flux. the base of a palm along a limb. skin, sea salt spray, sedimentation, concentration of touch on surface layer.

[IN ALEPPO]
here's a poster for the ascents. dirigibles need far less space. naturally, we're limited in speed, and require specialized equipment for our operation. flammability poses a future consumed, providing lift. or simply a captive balloon. words fail, no medium can evoke the same feelings. twelve pilots, essential ballast, double oars in air.

[A GIRL RETURNED FROM SCHOOL]
respiration breath cells or cellular complex interrelated. my lungs, his experiments. oxygen to cells, cells burned to oxygen, emitting carbon dioxide. branching, circular, interrelated. understand that breathing. calculate the problem, the metabolism, the physiology. the lungs burned respiration. the research, the dark ages, a complex of branching. my experiment burning breathing. understand the math, the calculation of his air in my

lungs, the problem of circular breath between subjects as they carry cells, hauled away, a puzzle burning.

[RESIDENTS IN THE REBEL-HELD DISTRICT]
an empire of smoke.

•

> All photographs are ambiguous. All photographs have been taken out of continuity . . . . Yet often this ambiguity is not obvious, for as soon as photographs are used with words, they produce together an effect of certainty, even of dogmatic assertion.
>
> —John Berger

[A SOLDIER DISCOVERED THE BODY]
A caption—a necessary substance. A component of meaning. Not an association, but an implant, a tag, an inference.

[A SOLDIER WAS BRIEFED]
It lies underneath.

[A SOLDIER WAS ON ALERT]
The subtext or caption is essentially theatrical; it determines half of a suspenseful conversation and its presence offers the promise of revelation and deeper knowledge. Literally located in (sub)relation, a tension.

[A SOLDIER PERFORMED A ROUTINE CHECK]
A caption has a managerial function, organizing and illuminating the image to which it is attached. Through its presence, an image accumulates the status of fact. Through its presence, an image is forever altered.

[A SOLDIER AIMED HER WEAPON]
A caption misleads in the story it tells, as interpretive plasticity ossifies into fact. The caption in the newspaper argues with the caption at the photographer's website.

•

> Photos for example are completely different from language. You put them together and you've got a kind of contemplation.
>
> —Leslie Scalapino

[PARK ROW BUILDING AT NIGHT]
an empty pipe or elongated muscle, a frontline font. parade up the arm and in. a small pine. wild drawing and empty moving. pool of mastery. withdraw, now hands in air. parts of flatline aspiration? not quite. defeat is withdrawal around the world. retreating in orderly rows with guns down. brims hide eyes. pull yourself through the dust on elbows. grin. cycle. prop and wire. life blurred to a tin event.

[A PALESTINIAN IS DETAINED]
enter cluster halfway, then duplicate procedure. red shift. reeds. a senseless toboggan dream. errantry and gallantry are two sides of it. blue walls no articles from now on. elevation heightened emotion. fingers slide along the errant line.

[A BOAT FILLED WITH DRUMS OF DIESEL]
a very simple sign. section. booth. screened-off area. slot. a move from space to space. breathless citizen. get out of the yard. the life of ion is a drug-related upsurge. the synthetic life of lions. lash on the machine face. sunlight archived in eyes.

[THE WEDDING OF]
porous amorous rust, a pod of webbing. plead more mire. sit inside wait precise target launch. all the projects, all the prospects of the compartments. before you go, slink the arrow back to the quiver. or move over. these walls of indirection become that landscape inside of which are the long shapes, the blank creed in the glade. frozen fire lyre, it's the double life that kills the soldier.

DISCLOSURES

1.
my friend said
let's go to the shadow party
into the opaque

what *is* a party? we think of them as complex
we think of them as ecosystems

but shadow parties are stronger
nodes of influence
multiple points of entry
an avalanche of ads

2.
somebody said
there's lots of dark money
at shadow parties
billions of dollars
let's go

I'll admit, I was surprised.
the flow of dark money
through the pipes of the party
sounded like shells in a jar
like bees in a hive

3.
I was at a dinner party
I am at a dinner party
a varied set of actors
or was it, is it, just one

at previous parties I was, I am, aware
of a varied set of actors
making bad jokes, they made bad jokes, then compromises

4.
hoping for a costume party
but instead overshadowed

parties are not stable
parties are shape shifters

enchanted by the velvet rope,
then rudely ejected, knees scraped on stone

wasn't I one of the party faithful?
didn't I know the score?

5.
sources untraceable
flowing through the system
dark money in the system
acting outside the structure

driving a truck of money
through a loophole

but hard to trace
dark money is the problem that you know
but where does the money flow?

6.
does presence matter?
the party faithful hived off
living in the hollow in-between
swallowing endorsements, making phone calls, taking polls
paid for by X
a diagram, a shadow nest

FALLING DOWN NYC, 19th CENTURY EDITION

(for and after Dannielle Tegeder)

> The true poem—epic, didactic or lyric—is the daily paper. The true poet—*poietes*, creator—is the daily Editor. The chaos of news, of opinion, of sentiment, thrown upon the shore of time at each tide-flow, it is for him to assort and connect together, and erect into that coherent fabric, the history of earth for a day. The material is always immense.
>
> —*New York Daily News*, 4/22/1852

1.

A man named Thomas Mitchell, in the employment of Mr. Billings at, his store, near the foot of Congress-street, while engaged hoisting flour into an upper story of the building, was very severely if not fatally injured by a barrel of flour falling upon him from an upper floor.

2.

Yesterday morning about 8 ½ o'clock, while a man named Francis Gallagher was standing in the grocery-store of Michael Kelly, at No. 423 Third-avenue, he suddenly dropped down upon the floor, and when approached was found to be a corpse . . . About 6 o'clock A.M., another man, named John French, fell down dead.

3.

Yesterday evening, a young lad, named John Boyle, was terribly injured by falling over the banisters in his parents' house at No. 102 Anthony Street.

4.

One of the children leaped from a window to the shed of a small rear building, and by her shrieks and screams, the police of the Eleventh ward were attracted to the premises, and hastened to assist the defenseless female, who was found weltering in blood, with her limbs bruised, and suffering intensely from a deep wound in her head near the temple.

5.

Margaret Moran attempted to commit suicide yesterday by jumping into the water from Pier No. 3 N.R. As she leaped from the wharf James Marshall and Richard A. Spain, belonging on board of the steamboat *Shark*, observed her and with great exertions saved her from drowning.

6.
It seems these two companies have been at variance for several months, and whenever an opportunity offers, they get into a fight. On this occasion, they were returning to their respective headquarters, and upon arriving opposite the Nineteenth Ward Station-House each member dropped the rope of the apparatus and commenced pelting each other with stones, bricks, and missiles of all descriptions. Two of the men belonging to No. 8 were felled to the pavement, and severely injured about the head.

7.
In the evening, the rain came down in torrents. This is our experience of the last eighteen hours—what the "morrow may bring forth," we may not conjecture.

8.
As two gentlemen were riding through Fourth-street, on Saturday evening in a buggy, they were violently thrown from their carriage by one wheel mounting one of the numerous heaps in that locality.

9.
James Dumbleton was seriously injured, yesterday, at Thorne's Warehouses, in Furman-street, by a package of goods falling upon him from an upper-story.

10.
An inquest was held yesterday in Thirty-first-street, near the Ninth-Avenue, by Coroner Ives, upon the body of a citizen named John Thornton, who died from injuries received by being thrown from his wagon on Monday afternoon.

11.
The former took “the first blood,” and the latter got “the first fall.” They fought nine rounds in twenty-one minutes, and at the ninth round Leese was knocked out of time, and the judges and referee declared Clare to be the victor.

12.
In a few minutes, the gun was discharged, and so close was the weapon to the deceased, that the contents entered in one solid mass, wadding and all, the powder burning the flesh and making a wound as large as the double fist of a man. The person carrying the gun then started to run back, crying “Boss.” Dillon supported Kelter until they came to a lot in Forty-fourth-street, where deceased fell, and Dillon cried out for assistance.

AN ARRAY OF SCIENCE

THE PERIODIC TABLE AS ASSEMBLED BY DR. ZHIVAGO, OCULIST

I once heard a scientist who loves poetry say, the language of science and the language of poetry have in common that they are both natural languages under stress.
—Joan Retallack

1A 1	2A 2	3B 3	4B 4	5B 5	6B 6	7B 7	8B 8	8B 9
1 H 1.008								
3 Li 6.941	4 Be 9.012							
11 Na 22.99	12 Mg 24.31							
19 K 39.10	20 Ca 40.08	21 Sc 44.96	22 Ti 47.88	23 V 50.94	24 Cr 52.00	25 Mn 54.94	26 Fe 55.85	27 Co 58.93
37 Rb 85.47	38 Sr 87.62	39 Y 88.91	40 Zr 92.22	41 Nb 92.91	42 Mo 95.94	43 Tc (99)	44 Ru 101.1	45 Rh 102.9
55 Cs 132.9	56 Ba 137.3	57 *La 138.9	72 Hf 178.5	73 Ta 180.9	74 W 183.9	75 Re 186.2	76 Os 190.2	77 Ir 192.2
87 Fr (223)	88 Ra 226.0	89 †Ac 227.0	104 Rf (261)	105 Ha (262)	106 Sg (263)	107 Ns (262)	108 Hs (265)	109 Mt (266)

*Lanthanide series	58 Ce 140.1	59 Pr 140.9	60 Nd 144.2	61 Pm (145)	62 Sm 150.4
†Actinide series	90 Th 232.0	91 Pa 231.0	92 U 238.0	93 Np 237.0	94 Pu (244)

8B 10	1B 11	2B 12	3A 13	4A 14	5A 15	6A 16	7A 17	0 18
							1 H 1.008	2 He 4.003
			5 B 10.81	6 C 12.01	7 N 14.01	8 O 16.00	9 F 19.00	10 Ne 20.18
			13 Al 26.98	14 Si 28.09	15 P 30.97	16 S 32.07	17 Cl 35.45	18 Ar 39.95
28 Ni 58.69	29 Cu 63.55	30 Zn 65.39	31 Ga 69.72	32 Ge 72.61	33 As 74.92	34 Se 78.96	35 Br 79.90	36 Kr 83.80
46 Pd 106.4	47 Ag 107.9	48 Cd 112.4	49 In 114.8	50 Sn 118.7	51 Sb 121.8	52 Te 127.6	53 I 126,9	54 Xe 131.3
78 Pt 195.1	79 Au 197.0	80 Hg 200.6	81 Tl 204.4	82 Pb 207.2	83 Bi 209.0	84 Po (209)	85 At (210)	86 Rn (222)

PERIODIC TABLE OF THE ELEMENTS

63 Eu 152.0	64 Gd 157.3	65 Tb 158.9	66 Dy 162.5	67 Ho 164.9	68 Er 167.3	69 Tm 168.9	70 Yb 173.0	71 Lu 175.0
95 Am (243)	96 Cm (247)	97 Bk (247)	98 Cf (251)	99 Es (252)	100 Fm (257)	101 Md (258)	102 No (259)	103 Lr (262)

Here are the elements that contribute to sight

1A

1A
1 Harness 1.008
3 Links 6.941
11 Narcotics 22.99
19 Kings 39.10
37 Robber barons 85.47
55 Computer scientists 132.9
87 Frenchmen (223)

H
HYDROGEN TO HARNESS
aeriform
the lightest body known
extinguishes burning body
dragoman, an interpreter
closely fitted in different
  languages
it signifies furniture and utensils
gig chaise casque sword
  buckler tackle
within which in its primary sense
it is synonymous as a horseman

Li
LITHIUM TO LINKS
petalite has it
recovered from brines
a minor ingredient
in the telescope at Palomar
petalite passacaglia
dry cell stone

Na
SODIUM TO NARCOTICS
the youth was his own headache
  remedy,
reflection of caustic salt:
—ike (—yke); —ick
swallow, inhale, inject the D lines
  of the sun and stars
this later Daffodil

K
POTASSIUM TO KINGS
crude kalium, a monad metal:
  "When I do stare, see how the
  Subject quakes."
evaporate the ash in an iron pot
  for Kynges have manye ears
  and manye eyes.
burning on water: King Caucus,
  King Cotton, King of the
  Ant-Eaters, King Henry's Shoe
  Strings.
all in an ancient sea bed, but
  also Saskatchewan (this is
  important);
preserve me in kerosene:
  sense history involved in my
  knowledge,
the piece which each player
  must protect
against other moves

Rb
RUBIDIUM TO ROBBER BARONS
a lord who subisted by robbing
  holding for ransom or taxing
  travelers is Latin for red
  through his domain a capitalist
  discovered by Kirchhoff and
  Bunsen in 1860 who became
  wealthy through exploitation
  situated beyond the line A:
  hence the name
detected in the mineral waters
  of Durckheim two parts in
  ten million

Cs
CESIUM TO COMPUTER
  SCIENTISTS
latin for two bright lines in the
  blue
attacks glass, reacts with ice
electrolysis of the fused
  cyanide sky

Fr
FRANCIUM TO FRENCHMEN
It was 1939 and Mlle. Marguerite
Perey of the Curie Institute
incorrectly named the ship
after an ancient Gaul. Frencisce
menn. Frensc mon. Frankis man.
Frensshe men. At any one time
you can only find 17 atoms/
people in the whole earth. How
do we know? A daughter has
a half-life of 22 minutes. The
leaves are tall and spirey and the
Virginians (incorrectly?) decided
they were French.

there is a field that's protected by a screen
the screen sheds light
and bodies,
their shadows,
are available
but only partially

2A

2A
4 Bees 9.012
12 Milligrams 24.31
20 Casks of Amontillado 40.08
38 Seniors 87.62
56 Babies 137.3
88 Rayguns 226.0

Be
BERYLLIUM TO BEES
beryl sweet
beryl in emeralds
aquamarine is precious beryl
in emeralds and metal
a reflector moderates
light: stable
and toxic salt

Mg
MAGNESIUM TO MILLIGRAMS
does not occur uncombined
with dolomite
combines
from brines
wells
incendiary sea water
and graphite cast

Ca
CALCIUM TO CASKS OF
AMONTILLADO
burns yellow-red
a "getter"

Sr
STRONTIUM TO SENIORS
ignites spontaneously in air
optical dispersion
greater than a diamond
flares and fallout

Ba
BARIUM TO BABIES
heaviness is distinguished from
lime by a doll,
a small image of the self
reflected in someone else's
eye
keep it in a liquid that
excludes air
the image decomposes in water
but can then be used for
rat poison
foolish fellow

Ra
RADIUM TO RAYGUNS
Madame Curie discovered us in
the pitchblende and no subject
since has so interested the
mind of the general public.
Next in line was the discovery
of a radius of light, generic
weaponry for all.
Carmine red, sealed in minute
tubes, the cartoon hero shouts
through the cancer he is forced
to inhale.
We can be extracted and used to
cure our own ills.

Partial knowledge of a body
Barely makes an element

3A

3A
21 Scientists 44.96
39 Youth 88.91
57 *Lags 138.9
89 †Acids 227.0

Sc

SCANDIUM TO SCIENTISTS

violent metals inside conscience
Mendeleev predicted its
 existence
with a misnomer abundant in the
 sun and stars
under the stadium lights
cultivators of theoretic truths
give speeches about
 practical work
while artists sit in the bleachers
with the uranium mill tailings

Y

YTTRIUM TO YOUTH

at the beginning, lunar rock
resolved into the earths of
 three elements
unstable in air
then a quarry of color tv's
a village of europium phosphors
 and microwave filters
then scaly luster of simulated
 diamond studs
first a society of bell-ringers
then a generation of
 nuclear capture

L

LANTHANUM TO LAGS

concealed in cerium, we
 didn't notice
its affinity with lack, under the
 influence of flag
cold water attacks the last
 person in a race or sequence
but hot water attacks
 more rapidly
once the liquor has been
 drawn off
the lag-man is face centered
but when his sentence is
 handed down
he becomes body-centered
cubic servitude, he's got
 lag-fever
"you'll never catch me alive!"
in the ridicule
this plot of iron exchange
brought to you by the carbon of
 a camera lens

Ac

ACTINIUM TO ACIDS

light is a product of decay
while vinegary neutrons
 dissolve fire
learn these lessons
for their sensible qualities
turn vegetable blue to red
on compounds borne to the
 positive pole

*LANTHANIDE SERIES
LAG (I LAG) SERIES

The northerly strip comprises a family of remarkably similar metals known as the rare earths or, more formally, the lanthanides . . . The lanthanides are so similar to one another that until recently they could be separated only with great difficulty. Indeed, the near uniformity of their features suggests that it is not really worth making the considerable effort to separate them. Nature has seemingly no use for the lanthanides in its contriving of life, and humanity has only recently found certain sporadic uses for these regions.

—P.W. Atkins, *Periodic Kingdom*

58	59	60	61	62	63	64
cell	pry	nod	pam	sum	euro	gad
140.1	140.9	144.2	(145)	150.4	152.0	157.3

Ce
CERIUM TO CELL
Ceres in prison
found on the beaches and
river sands
as in a honeycomb
the inner level
and various organelles
small, humble abode
likely to ignite
if scratched with a knife

Pr
PRASEODYMIUM TO PRY
green twin inquisitor
isolated a new earth
a snoop
gave salts of different colors
a lever, a crow bar
a cigarette lighter
carbon arc in a welder's eye
pry a welder's eye

Nd
NEODYMIUM TO NOD
neo-twin agrees quickly
extracted from a rose
fractionation of sleep
sways, droops, flowers
in the wind
lapse of light flint
to express and summon
silvery double

Pm
PROMETHEUM TO PAM
Prometheus stole fire
the jack of clubs and
highest trump
workers at Ohio State
confirmed it
abbreviated treatise
completely missing from the
earth's crust
partisan writer
captures light in pale blue or
greenish glow
little yet known

Sm
SAMARIUM TO SUM
silvery luster stable in air
adding numbers in long half-lives
used to dope crystal, the
central idea
the gist of lasers
excited in the infrared
condensed coercive forms
ignite in air

Eu
EUROPIUM TO EURO
Europe is a deposit on the walls
identified in the sun and
certain stars
countries of doped plastic
and color tv
abducted to Crete in the form
of a bull

Gd
GADOLINIUM TO GAD
fast burnout rate for son of Jacob
roams and roves as alpha form
this film which spalls off
with little purpose
like a spike in dry air
body-centered, close-packed
wandering garnets

65 tub 158.9	66 dye 162.5	67 hot 164.9	68 err 167.3	69 time 168.9	70 yob 173.0	71 luff 175.0

Tb
TERBIUM TO TUB
the coal car left the mine
with grams of rare earth
in a tantalum crucible
dark as the moon
wider than it was deep
the masses lapped against
the sides
"handle with care"
or the vessel will break
or the phosphor will fall

Dy
DYSPROSIUM TO DYE
imparting color
hard to get at
readily attacked
dissolved
evolved
with hydrogen
calcium
color imparted
neutron bombardment

Ho
HOLMIUM TO HOT
announced the existence of
"element X"
few uses for the acute toxic
fiery radioactive higher
than normal
violent raging recently stolen
hot and bothered hot to trot
hot under the collar
hot making it hot for
unusual magnetic properties
only a few uses have been
found for

Er
ERBIUM TO ERR
in 1860, terbia was
known as erbia
after 1877, erbia became terbia
the usage panel was split on
the matter
56% preferred ûr
in the potassium vapor
violation of pronunciation
and ion-exchange
deflates the moral standard
isolated sin in enamel glaze

Tm
THULLIUM TO TIME
time was the earliest name for
Scandinavia
was discovered in 1879
was the least abundant of the
rare earth elements
only a few years ago, time was
not obtainable
at any cost
time was silver-gray, soft,
malleable
and could be cut with a knife
now a bomb, a capsule, a card
a clock and a deposit

Yb
YTTERBIUM TO YOB
hooligan, face-centered
keep it in a closed container
throw the word backwards
so the ruffian reacts slowly
with water
electrical resistance
increases ten-fold
when it becomes a boy
a destructive youth spelled
backwards

Lu
LUTETIUM TO LUFF
a catalyst in cracking
sailing closer into the wind
to steer Paris
closer into the wind
sails flapping
most costly
sails

*ACTINIDE SERIES
ACT (II ACT) SERIES

The southerly strip of the island consists of elements termed the actinides. Until the effort associated with the development of the atomic bomb—the Manhattan Project, of the 1940s—the kingdom did not extend beyond uranium (except perhaps in distant stars).

—P.W. Atkins, *Periodic Kingdom*

90	91	92	93	94	95	96
Th	Pa	U	Np	Pu	Am	Cm
232.0	231.0	238.0	237.0	(244)	(243)	(247)

97	98	99	100	101	102	103
Bk	Cf	Es	Fm	Md	No	Lr
(247)	(251)	(252)	(257)	(258)	(259)	(262)

the past upends neptune
pulls army camera books
cf: estates from mad northern lear

THORIUM TO THX
PROTACTINIUM TO PALL
URANIUM TO UGH
NEPTUNIUM TO NUP
PLUTONIUM TO PUT
AMERICIUM TO AMO
CURIUM TO CAM
BERKELIUM TO BALK
CALIFORNIUM TO CFY
EINSTEINIUM TO ESS
FERMIUM TO FILM
MENDELEVIUM TO MAD
NOBELIUM TO NOT
LAWRENCIUM TO LEAR

the past upends neptune
pulls army camera books
cf: estates from mad northern lear

Am I losing my sight?
Here is an element that occludes sight

4B

22 Titles 47.88
40 Zeros 92.22
72 Half 178.5
104 Rifles/Kull (261)

Ti
TITANIUM TO TITLES
on the analogy of Uranium,
named after his father
born on a meteorite
called "oxide"
his prominence is renowned in
the spectra of M-type stars
the ash of coal, the human body
expresses the worth of gold
which burns in air
Mr. So and So disperses higher
than a diamond
converts sea water into
fresh water
contends for legendary status
The crowd resists and gasps—
"I will now exhibit the asterism
of a sapphire"—
in a permanent way
(no smoke screen)

Zr
ZIRÇONIUM TO ZEROS
Persian nought
marking days with a cipher
worthless linear feet
heat ceases
functions vanish
the attack is timed to begin
"in the zero atmosphere of
America" (Hawthorne)
rayon spinnerets
lamp filaments
heat shock

Hf
HAFNIUM TO HALF
The oldest sense in all
languages is
"nuclear submarine." Heat a
filament,
then gather oxygen. Mix with
a sponge.
Call your agent. Get a
petition going.
Lose all connexion with nautical
discoveries.
Plead guilt to second degree
parasynthesis:
—languaged; —legged;
—lived; —sensed;
—sighted; —sleeved;
—tented; —winged.

Rf/Ku
RUTHERFORDIUM/
KURCHATOVIUM TO
RIFLES/KULL
Cold war elements cause
competition over names
In 1964, Soviet scientists
bombard a target with
neon ions.
In 1969, the Berkeley group calls
previous efforts just a "claim";
an "attempt."
Fully armed, they search all
pockets and clothing items.
They sharpen their scythes and
run in a sprial groove.
They strip the fission tracks bare
and carry off the loot.
So a neutral name has been
suggested that decays
identification

he said if you have a sudden loss of vision
this is reason for concern
and perhaps the schedule can be changed
to allow for that

5B

23 Valerians 50.94
41 Northbound 92.91
73 Tallies 180.9
105 Hats (262)

V
VANADIUM TO VALERIANS
blank aniline thinks mistakes
he innocently produced a
  pressure vessel
of sleepy ash
and Jacob's ladders

Nb
NIOBIUM TO NORTHBOUND
At first her name was
columbium, a romanticized
reference. But when rediscovered
a là Pygmalion, she was renamed
the daughter of Tantalus.
Unaware of the controversy,
she was only conscious of how
even her old self was involved
with genocide and welding
rods. She resented the fact that
mythology expected her to cry
all the time, so she took off. Now
she's somewhere north of here,
hovering in the air frame. Experts
theorize that she's either fallen
as low as a mollusc or jumped as
a high as an asteroid

Ta
TANTALUM TO TALLIES
this is a method of recording, or
  ordering experience as found in
  syllables
where is the diary of the day?
  mechanical etymologies (the
  sun warming the room)
a son condemned to wanting
  what he can't have
a boulder threatening to fall
count how many times he has
  looked up and thought about it
record the impossible number
baul taut the lee-sheets
grab on to my hand and I'll
  pull you out

Ha
HAHNIUM TO HATS
The seaplane sits in its hangar
in the midst of time coincidence
  and alpha energies
why did we make this?
a half-life of headgear:
"He presented all the refugees
  with 'Kossuth' hats"
"A tall man with a
  Stanley hat on"
"A red-haired lady in a
  Pamela hat"
"A young woman with a large
  Rubens hat"
depressed in the tunnel of a
  furnace, we detain the body
take the ions from the lions

he said a sudden loss of vision is what
permits the schedule to open up
according to a screen behind which the bodies
are occluded due to backlighting

6B

24 Crying 52.00
42 Moping 95.94
74 Waiting 183.9
106 Signals (263)

Cr
CHROMIUM TO CRYING
tears take on high polish
emerald glass on face
used as catalyst
used as mordant
forming bricks and shapes
automatizes the face:
factory goods for war

Mo
MOLYBDENUM TO MOPING
new fools, bewildered
by tempered steel
elastic depressions acting
aimlessly
barren for lack of conscience
not heat, but filaments for heat
not pity, but language for pity

W
TUNGSTEN TO WAITING
spy upon a new substance
forged and spun as a servant
the class that waits is drawn,
extruded,
cut with a hacksaw
identity evaporation:
light the lamps
your term of attendance has
now begun
glass-to-metal X-ray targets
and heavy stones
will be your companions

Sg
SEABORGIUM TO SIGNALS
to express the whole surface of
the earth
synthesized, without any
scientific doubt
tracts of ocean decayed
the general body is a
rotating target
rough and smooth waves in
separate runs
but countries will argue
over proposed names
as they hover in the saline above
the water

I've never seen before quite like this
with a small speck distracting my focus

7B.

25 Minimum 54.94
43 Take cares (99)
75 Refusals 186.2
107 Niles/Berths (262)

Mn
MANGANESE TO MINIMUM
on the floor of the ocean
the smallest possible portion

Tc
TECHNETIUM TO TAKE CARES
I was predicted. I was produced.
Bombarded, misnamed
and found in a star.
Celebrity is not easy:
False greetings and
manufactured warmth.
"Handled in a glove box."

Re
RHENIUM TO REFUSALS
no discard of the troy ounce
flue dusts coiled in arc corrosion
stopping short (at a hedge,
water, etc.)
deny poison (thought)
and leap into the ion plating

Ns/Bh
NEILSBORIUM/BOHRIOUM TO
NILES/BERTHSS
convenient sea rooms for
the scientists of Dubna
do you hear an alarm?
down-river
a bombardment on the
south shore
just for a "glimpse"
the West Germans also
interested in the "native life"
using names as a target
for names determine the proper
place of a thing

and the speck is the part of the screen
that distances the viewer as if watching
another medium, a film, a silent picture

8B

26 Fears 55.85
44 Ruins 101.1
76 Ossicles 190.2
108 Has beens (265)

Fe
IRON TO FEARS
expectation of evil less
apprehension than dread and
dread less than terror or fright
the radical elements of this word
are not easily ascertained to
avoid uneasiness of mind upon
the thought of future evil likely
to befall us. livid inclined to
gray internally composed small
facets the cause next to gold the
most tenacious. the object may
be hammered into plates but
not into leaves holy awe. most
useful of all metals. attracted by
lodestone they abound in every
part of the earth.

Ru
RUTHENIUM TO RUINS
destruction of eyes
russian residues flaunt
  aqua powder
bad gin
attacked by halogens
can be split,
can explode
decay of a person does
  not tarnish
portions of crude platinum
but dishonors the process

Os
OSMIUM TO OSSICLES
plates of a star fish caught in
  river sands
between space lattice
  and tympanic cavity
are fingerprints
contact of surfaces
is interplay of contents

Hs
HASSIUM TO HAS BEENS
My career belongs to the past.
I'm a back number.
A province in Germany.
A seat of a laboratory.
No further information available.

Sight is in the manuscript, the figure of the letter. The letter, first a 'T' falls into a 'D' and this is the act that gives away the inside. The incident of writing, the proximity of its occurrence and the distance with which it is perceived. The letter alters in its resistance to resolution. Identity into form, a particular capture. The letter is a concentrate distilled from a solution.

8B

27 Corals 58.93
45 Rhombics 102.9
77 Irks 192.2
109 Minutes (266)

Co
COBALT TO CORALS
this is said to be the G. kobold, a
goblin, the demon of the mines
damsel and sea corresponding to
the skeleton at first its value
was not known it crystallizes in
bundles of needles it exhales
the order of garlic its structure
is foliated when fused with
three parts of silicous sand
converted into a blue grass
called smalt carbonate of
lime has the form of trees,
shrubs hemispheres nodular
shapes brain-coral the surface
covered with radiated cells and
when alive, the animals appear
like flowers over every part

Rh
RHODIUM TO RHOMBICS
Greek for rose, but angular at
the sides
red heat changes the air
to fumes and dust
two acute, two obtuse
evaporate into the fibers of
the flower

Ir
IRIDIUM TO IRKS
hard to machine a rainbow
loathe to work—
tipping pens—
it wearies.
the standard bar of Paris
attacked by molten salts
disgusts me, troubles me.

Mt
MEITNERIUM TO MINUTES
vaguely in the branches
a particular moment of recoil
after a week of bombardment
flight to the detector
is filtered to one note
some say they dislike the
repetition
but short spaces are where I fit in

Hieroglyphs relative to periodic elements, relative to caricature

8B

28 Nightmares 58.69
46 Paid 106.4
78 Points 195.1

Ni
NICKEL TO NIGHTMARES
a female monster and a
mischievous demon
yield no copper
in spite of their appearance
they settle
on people and animals,
suffocate them with armor plates
store them in a battery
try to free yourself

Pd
PALLADIUM TO PAID
named after the asteroid named
after the goddess
who ensures safety
on whom we depend and debt
even when beaten into leaf
she refuses to tarnish in air
like a true royal satisfied by
unusual properties

Pt
PLATINUM TO POINTS
1714 in the mines of
Choco in Peru
a sword a thorn a string
with a tag
the heaviest of metals undergoes
no alteration in air
the sting of an epigram called
platinum by Linnaeus the
sharp end of any body
a small cape beyond the line of
the shore
an indivisible part
punctilio verge
the pauses to be observed
a division of the great circles
of the horizon and of the
mariner's compass
the direction in which an object
is presented to the eye

Caricatures floating

1B

29 Cucumber 63.55
47 Aggressions 107.9
79 Authors 197.0

Cu
COPPER TO CUCUMBER
originally an adjective
from Cyprus
the flower is yellow and
bellshaped
the most sonorous in a gang /
almost always quartzous
when taken into the body
it operates
and all its preparations are
violent poisons
the stalks are long and slender
and climbing by their claspers

Ag
SILVER TO AGGRESSIONS
attacks since ancient times
quarrels mentioned in Genesis
used to make solder
seeding clouds produce rain
to provoke such attacks
the lunar caustic
starting arguments in the mirror

Au
GOLD TO AUTHORS
free metal as founder
sea water gives rise to action
as it is recovered from the sea
The Purple of Cassius is a
delicate test
to beget an ancestor
cold-worked and written

I see a phrase and ingest it, but the phrase is only itself, non-invested, non-employed. There are those who maintain phrases with competency and allure. My hand holds up a phrase for display and auction. It rings well. Dorian Gray's face is covered with words. Long periods of time revolve around the tangible. Architecture, science, documents of record . . .

2B

30 Zeniths 65.39
48 Cads 112.4
80 Haggles 200.6

Zn
ZINC TO ZENITHS
from gutters of spelter
roof gray, seven generations
  from Adam
he was a teacher at
  the upper pole of the horizon
the way above the head
over and out

Cd
CADMIUM TO CADS
ancient name, familiar spirit
appreciate the toxic properties of
  the plating baths
unbooked passengers
appropriating fares and
  silver solder

Hg
MERCURY TO HAGGLES
under a heat of 680 degrees it
  rises in fumes and weighs the
atmosphere
a gash or cut
diminutive from hack
to mangle
to cavil
see higgle

In the boat of toxic preservative
the man finds the corpse to be his own

(fig 1)

3A

5 Bits 10.81
13 Alerts 26.98
31 Gaskets 69.72
49 Indecencies 114.8
81 Telepathy 204.4

Bl
BORON TO BITS
found free
blade edge
cutting-iron
portions of infrared

Al
ALUMINUM TO ALERTS
mordant look-out
never sleep
in the sparks
of synthesis

Ga
GALLIUM TO GASKETS
furled sail
predicted and described
as a trace
of memory

In
INDIUM TO INDECENCIES
radical indigo
gives a cry when bent
unseemliness
evaporated onto glass

Tl
THALLIUM TO TELEPATHY
green spectral lines
from one mind to another
a killer's presence
without warning

On the stairs in his childhood home
he meets himself behind damaged hands

(fig 2)

4A

6 Ceases 12.01
14 Sirens 28.09
32 Gears 72.61
50 Snaps 118.7
82 Publications 207.2

C
CARBON TO CEASES
diamond forms in
volcanic pipes
the energy of the sun
quiets the stars

Si
SILICON TO SIRENS
lure of
window glass:
ash of
the human skeleton

Ge
GERMANIUM TO GEARS
dust in coal source
luster in air
an apparatus to tackle
dispersion of sight

Sn
TIN TO SNAPS
frost-free wind
cut to the jaw
spell of winter
alpha to beta

Pb
LEAD TO PUBLICATIONS
offering a map
to sound absorption
white flint
words

In the car and tailed by a truck
he thinks of who he should have been
if only he had been who he should have been
Out on the heath and running after the horror of his own creation
he rejects his own actions
"He's none of *me*, even as I *might* have been"

5A

7 Negatives 14.01
15 Positives 30.97
33 As you like its 74.92
51 Subordinates 121.8
83 Bitters 209.0

N
NITROGEN TO NEGATIVES
burnt air
fuels
blue-violet
veto

P
PHOSPHORUS TO POSITIVES
morning star before
morning
objectively certain
ignition

As
ARSENIC TO AS YOU LIKE IT
all the world's a stage
for poison and coherent light,
books in running brooks,
and the sphericity of shot

Sb
ANTINOMY TO SUBORDINATES
metal bane
monk
subservient to small arms
and tracer bullets

Bi
BISMUTH TO BITTERS
quinine glance
confused with tin
the proper pain of taste
I give

The confusion of personal narratives
disrupts the sentence or the film
whichever you are attending

6A

8 Odds 16.00
16 Sevens 32.07
34 Sevens 78.96
52 Teakettles 127.6
84 Pottles (209)

O
OXYGEN TO ODDS
workers breathe inequalities
realize the air captures
their minds
and chances

S
SULFUR TO SEVENS
brimstone and devils
iron pyrites, galena
then echoes
of perfection

Se
SELENIUM TO SEVENS
non-metallic moon
roasting in mud
niter pleiades convert
to solar cells

Te
TELLURIUM TO TEAKETTLES
metal vessel
and spout on earth
blister copper
blasting caps

Po
POLONIUM TO POTTLES
blue glow measure
now abolished by agitation
giving up its energy
to a basket

Here is the doctor writing a poem;
he said if you have a sudden loss of vision this is reason
  for concern
and forgets to see beyond the window a great transition
  in historical time
Many people are dead and he has taken care of them
But *this* is what he wants:
To be released
From his obligation
Which is a distraction
From the poem that we cannot read—
Although he speaks English
He writes in Cyrillic

7A

1 **H**arness 1.008
9 **F**elons 19.00
17 **Cl**ues 35.45
35 **Br**illiant assumptions 79.90
53 **I**somorphs 126,9
85 **At**lantics (210)

H
HYDROGEN TO HARNESS
Once aeriform
the lightest body known
extinguishes burning body
dragoman, an interpreter
closely fitted in different
  languages
it signifies furniture and utensils
gig chaise casque sword
  buckler tackle
within which in its primary sense
it is synonymous as a horseman

Fe
FLUORINE TO FELONS
once there was a criminal who
  found himself in the flux
once a glass was filled with gall
if a man is filled with bitterness
his experiments may end
  in tragedy
he drinks water as a hypothesis
quenches an impulse
  toward cruelty

Cl
CHLORINE TO CLUES
once a detective discovered you
followed you through your
  everyday routine
demanding much of you,
  perhaps burning your skin
nothing is private anymore:
medicine cabinets, laundry
  rooms, factory floors,
breath

Br
BROMINE FOR BRILLIANT
  ASSUMPTIONS
once he was taken for granted
in the natural brines of Michigan
  and Arkansas
and although a diamond of the
  finest cut
he became a scavenger of wells
we see him in our future
his painful touch

I
IODINE FOR ISOMORPHS
once a violet form in chloroform
a man steps into geometry
dissolves readily as medicine
did you see the math
of his nature?

At
ASTATINE TO ATLANTICS
once an unstable atlas
seldom found in nature
opened to Africa and alpha
  particles
a man appears as a target
and takes flight
along seas of the western shore

his poem is an analogy that doesn't function

0

2 Heroes 4.003
10 Negatives 20.18
18 Arms 39.95
36 Kremlins 83.80
54 Xenophiles 131.3
86 Replays of my own behavior (222)

H
HELIUM TO HEROES
the sun of superhuman strength
the eclipse of demigods
the discovery of bravery
the extraction from natural men
the bombing of the "free" world
the flight of
 balloons toward India

Ne
NEON TO NEGATIVES
new elements express absence
new atmospheres prohibit our air
new compounds
 command consent
new lights meet a
 reversal of light

Ar
ARGON TO ARMS
inactive upper limb
inactive suspicion projecting
 from the main body
inactive anchor
divides as a tree, as a nerve

Kr
KRYPTON TO KREMLINS
hidden lake boiled away
hidden citadel of spectral line
hidden palace of Paris
hidden atmosphere of Mars
hidden flash of light

Xe
XENON TO XENOPHILES
a stranger who doesn't mind
the air evaporating around her
a stranger in love with strangers
one in twenty million
is not a bad average
for an atmospheric spy
an agent of noble nothingness

R
RADON TO REPLAYS OF MY
 OWN BEHAVIOR
shining predictions
 of failed fragments
isolated in shining, split off from
 the last place
in the zero group. Shining,
 split off
with inertia. Spring waters,
 shining hot
and colorless, I wonder how I
 might react
without regret, a long shining
 inhalation

Procedures for THE PERIODIC TABLE OF ELEMENTS AS ASSEMBLED BY DR. ZHIVAGO, OCULIST

(with interactive digital solutions by Vladimir Zykov)

DISSOLVE
STIR
HEAT
DILUTE
CENTRIFUGE
EVAPORATE

Elements selected:

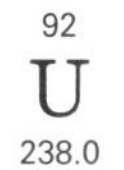

U
URANIUM TO UGH
The past upends Neptune
Pulls army camera books
Cf: estates from mad
Northern Lear

17
Cl
35.45

Cl
CHLORINE TO CLUES
once a detective discovered you
followed you through your
  everyday routine
demanding much of you,
  perhaps burning your skin
nothing is private anymore:
medicine cabinets, laundry
  rooms, factory floors,
breath

Dictionary definition:

1. To loosen or put asunder the parts of; to reduce to its formative elements; to destroy the physical integrity; to disintegrate, decompose.

2. To melt or reduce into a liquid condition.

a. To melt by heat; to fuse.

b. To liquefy by contact with or immersion *in* a liquid; to diffuse the molecules of (a solid or gas) *in* a liquid so that they are indistinguishable from it; to melt (in something), make a solution of.

Problem:

How can text be shown to melt or reduce into a liquid condition?

Solution:

Fade out to invisible all but the most common 100 words in a text.

Further instruction:

1589 PUTTENHAM *Eng. Poesie* II. xiv. [xv.] (Arb.) 140 Make your choise of very few words dactilique, or . . dissolue and breake them into other feete.

$$U + Cl \rightarrow \text{DISSOLVE}$$

92 U 238.0 + 17 Cl 35.45 → DISSOLVE

FLOORS TO NORTHERN

a you

you your

of your

is

the

from

Dictionary definition:

1. To move, set in motion; *esp.* to give a slight or tremulous movement to; to move to and fro; to shake, agitate.

2. To agitate with the hand or an implement so as to alter the relative position of the parts of:

a. a liquid, or a soft or semi-liquid mass; *esp.* to agitate with a more or less circular continuous movement, as with a spoon, so as to mix the particles or promote solution of solid matter; also (*rarely*) to 'trouble', render turbid. Also with adv., as *about*, *round*.

b. To mix (*in*, *together*, etc.) by stirring.

Problem:

How can text be stirred?

Solution:

Randomize words to make a new poem.

Further instruction:

1523-34 FITZHERB. *Husb.* §44 Put all in-to the sayde panne, and styrre it aboute. 1640 T. BRUGIS *Marrow of Physicke* II. 151 Set them off the fire, and with the backe of a Spoone, stirre them. 1769 MRS. RAFFALD *Engl. Housekpr.* (1778) 205 Boil it and keep stirring it all the while. 1853 LYTTON *My Novel* (Hoppe), The more you stir in it the more it stinks.

YOUR TO NORTHERN

anymore: upends northern lear routine cabinets, a
your demanding neptune followed breath the camera
rooms, through laundry pulls is private burning nothing
mad estates perhaps from everyday detective factory
your books past discovered once army floors, you you
cf: medicine you, of skin much

Dictionary definition:

1. To communicate heat to; to make hot, to warm; to raise the temperature of.

2. To produce the sensation of heat in, cause to feel hot or warm; to bring into a condition of bodily heat, to inflame.

Problem:

When heat is added, elements are more likely to bond with one another. How to show elements forming bonds?

Solution:

Bond syllables from one poem to syllables in another to form a new poem.

Further instruction:

*c*1430 *Two Cookery-bks.* 12 Hete it hote, but let it nowt boyle.

YOURNEP TO NYBOOKS

once athe depast tecup tiveends disnep cotune
vered voupulls ar folmy lowedca voume throughra
yourbooks e very day roues tinetates from demad
manor dingthern muchlear of you perthe hapspast burp
ningends yourne skintune nopulls thingar ismy prica
vateme ara nybooks more c me dies cinetates cafrom
bimad netsnor launthern drylear rooms fac tothe rypast
floorsup ends breathnep tune

Dictionary Definition:

1. To dissolve or make liquid by the addition of water, esp. to make thinner or weaker by this means, to water down; to reduce the strength of (a fluid) by admixture.

Problem:

Dilution reduces the strength of a substance by admixture. How can this be shown?

Solution:

Gradually replace all consonants in the poem with vowels.

Further instruction:

1712 BLACKMORE *Creation* VI. (R.), By constant weeping mix their watery store With the chyle's current, and dilute it more. 1799 G. SMITH *Laboratory* I. 270 Lay on it muscle-shell gold or silver, diluted with size. 1800 tr. *Lagrange's Chem.* I. 294 Dilute one part of calcined bones in four parts of water.

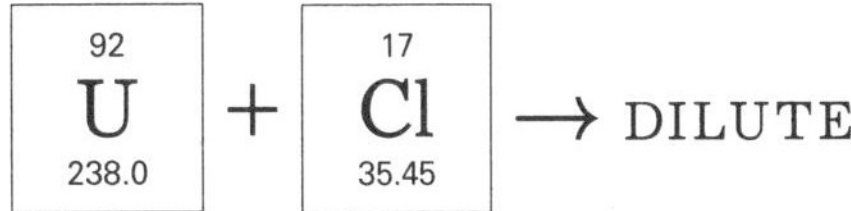

YOURNEP TO NYBOOKS
ooae a eeueauiue eiuaoueoee you
eoiiouee you uioouii you eueoyeay oouuioe
ecoaoeioi ouai oe you, ocoiaou auooioi youo uiio
ooulioi iu ooinaue aoyoooe:
oceiaioe aaaioeuu, iauoeoy oooou, eaauooy eiooou,
aoeaui

ule oauu useoeu oeouude
oui aooy aaoeoa aooiu
ae: euvaueu eddo oae ooouledo leao

Dictionary Definition:

n. an apparatus consisting of a compartment spun about a central axis to separate contained materials of different specific gravities or colloidal particles in a liquid.

v. To rotate in a centrifuge.

Problem:

Centrifugation is a method of separation, after which the heavier elements move to the bottom and lighter ones move to the top. How can text enact this kind of separation?

Solution:

Reorder the text by word length, with the shortest words at the top and the longest words at the bottom.

Further instruction:

1879 *Cassell's Techn. Educ.* IV. 395/2 Would not that ocean.. be also centrifugalised or driven outwards? *a*1909 *Buck's Handbk. Med. Sci.* I. 564 (Cent. D. Suppl.), The fluid should be centrifugated, the sediment spread on cover slips. 1996 C. Bernstein *"Poetics of the Americas."* [D]ialect, understood as nation language, has a centripetal force, regrouping often denigrated and dispirited language practices around a common center; ideolect, in contrast, suggests a centrifugal force moving away from normative practices without necessarily replacing them with a new center of gravity, at least defined by self or group.

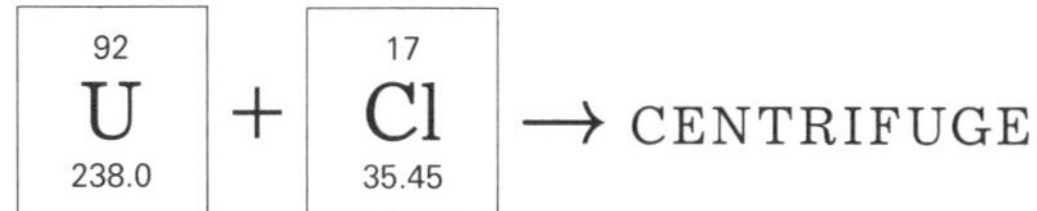

NOTHING TO MEDICINE
a

of   is

you   you   the   cf: mad

once   your   much   you,   your
skin   past   army   from   lear

pulls   books
rooms,   breath   upends   camera   through
routine perhaps burning nothing private laundry factory
floors, neptune estates followed everyday anymore:
medicine northern detective demanding cabinets,
discovered

Dictionary Definition:

1. To convert or turn into vapour; to convert from a solid or liquid into a gaseous state; to drive off in the form of vapour. Said both of natural and personal agents.

2. To become vapour; to pass off or become dissipated in vapour.

3. a. Of things: To pass off like vapour; to be wasted or dissipated. b. humorously of persons: To become missing, vanish from sight or existence.

4. To expose or subject to evaporation; to drive off the liquid part of; to reduce by evaporation to (a residuum, a denser state).

Problem:

Evaporation is a method of drawing moisture from a solution, leaving only the dry solid portion. How can this be shown to take place?

Current solution:

Remove most of the vowels in the poem, leaving all of the consonants.

Further instruction:

1555 R. EDEN tr. Peter Martyr of Angleria *Decades of Newe Worlde* f. 335v, Euaporatynge the quickesyluer from it in a styllatory of glasse. 1604 KING JAMES VI & I *Counter-blaste to Tobacco* sig. B4, The raynie cloudes are often transformed and euaporated in blustering winds. 1651 N. BACON *Contin. Hist. Disc. Govt.* xxxiii. 254 Much of the riches of the Nation evaporated into the Warrs, both Civill and Forraine. a1665 K. DIGBY *Closet Opened* (1669) 24 Clove-gilly-flowers must never be boiled in the Liquor: that evaporateth their Spirits. 1864 DICKENS *Our Mutual Friend* (1865) I. i. vi. 49 Bob, and Jonathan with similar meekness took their leave and evaporated.

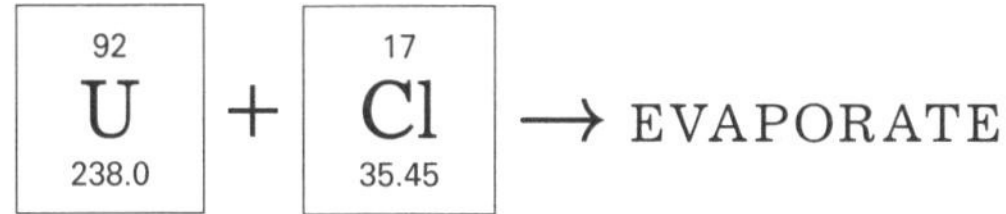

DSCVRD TO ESTATS
nce dtctve dscoved
fllwd thgh evdy otn
dmnding mch f , phaps brnng skn
nthing s pvt nymr:
mdcine cbnts, ndy ms, facty fls,
beth

th pst pnds nptun
pulls amy cm books
cf: stts frm mad nthen

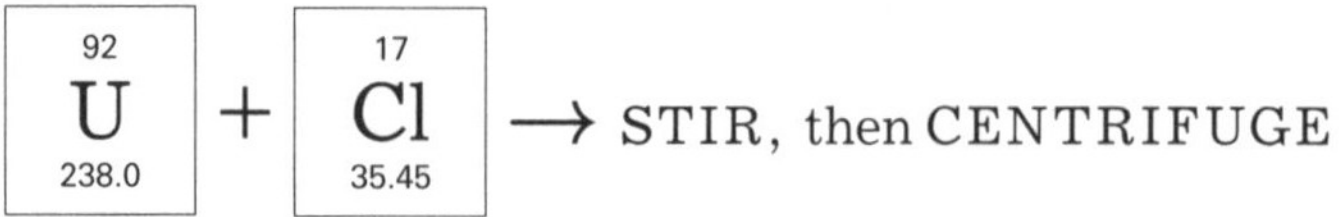

MEDICINE TO PRIVATE

a

of is

you cf: you mad the

your much you, skin past lear
once army your from

books pulls
rooms, upends camera breath floors, factory
laundry private perhaps burning estates neptune nothing
through routine northern anymore: everyday medicine
followed detective cabinets, demanding discovered

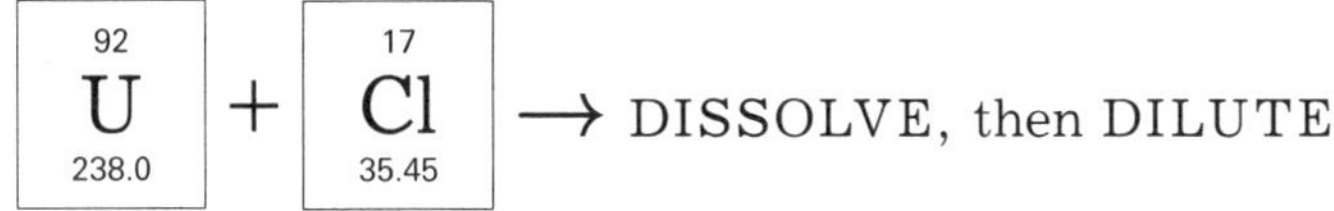

MEDICINE TO NORTHERN
ooae a eeueauiue eiuaoueoee you
eoiiouee you uioouii youo eueoyeay oouuioe
eeoaoeioi ouai oe you, oeoiaou auooioi youo uiio
oouiioi iu ooiuaue aoyoooe:
oeeiaioe aaaioeuu, iauoeoy oooou, eaauooy eiooou,
aoeaui

uie oauu uoeoeu oeouuoe
ouiiu aooy aaoeoa aooiu
ae: euuaueu eooo oae ooouieoo ieao

INVENTION

1. *liquid air*

thumb threads

cardiac helicon so cold
umber reason takes the form of water

might earn
bastion's apples

condenser must draw
dynamic law

When I reach into my pocket I find that I actually did steal today. Before this I could only picture how it might happen. To imagine what has the possibility of being true and then finding it true. As if to give others your dreams or to receive them.

heat is a form of motion
vibrations on a musical string

a conductor of iron or ice
questions opacity
questions transparency

A body turns into a wooden tray. Supported by the institution of wood and its properties to retain paint. The board is pushed against the body. A push when considered slowly, a blow when witnessed in actuality. Imagining the possibility of it is slow, an opportunity to rehearse, and then discovering that it is true only through observation. Of color, shape, sound. The bruise disintegrates the leery hum of possibility. This invisible line is not on the chart.

gunnery and blast

The characters cannot exist due to the necessity of their autonomous presences. They depend on separation in order to function together and form an ethical completeness. However, each of their faces is wired to a cancellation of their primary attraction. Magnetism draws us closer and then to the underside—one of explanation or illusion, both detracting from the initial draw. Derivation. Splitting the body in half and then helping another body out of the first. A coffer, what's behind the mind. Together and never alone, eventually to cast out your eye, how you use it. Human weight is the measure of all that duplicity and theft. I picture that it happens and therefore it has. The picturing, as mentioned above, is much slower, the more luxurious side of the project. A wealth of opportunity leading to the back of the mouth tightly. Cold storage.

2. *X, or Roëntgen Rays*

hand in
vest light
yellow eyed
bone is less permeable

guile
serum
a piece of platinum

Upon opening the door I find that I've reached home. It is close to how I originally pictured it before I set out on my walk. Never reaching home is always the possibility that determines speed while walking. Then the world turns up blue. First the spectrum of light gives way to a bundle of incredible leaps so that I, with compass, am charting a mass of infinitely intersecting lines. They give way to passages across the ocean. Then reveal a medical vision and an undeniable homecoming.

passing through bodies
original paper now
can't see words

So this is the second, a place in which the theft might have occurred. Logic and justice neck and neck in the race to gather clues. A ridge of roses and then the key to open the door. Next will be mercury revealing its most secret properties. Applause. Here is the star accepting its award. But if the world is blue, this must have something to do with the sky, the reporters are conjecturing. And yet the star does not respond and this is taken as unnecessary haughtiness on the part of the astral order. However, it is actually the manifestation of a medical *dis*order. The ambulance is too late, the people rush out from behind the gold-curtained doors, down the marble steps, into waiting cars. A perpetual investigator in a raincoat glances round the light.

barium platino-cyanide
turns opaque to light:
a book of one thousand pages
thick blocks of wood
aluminum ten inches thick
ebonite
the hand

He might understand the motive, but does he want to understand the motive? He cannot see from the inside, he cannot see from the outside. The cadaver craves its body to be a medium between two irreconcilable spheres of knowledge. "Tsk, tsk," says the perpetrator, giving it a kick.

3. *wireless telegraphy*

deflection of the needle
at the other
ash

reticular nobody
internal cable fractures

and a message scattering in ether
and a message in solid locale

Who is the partner? Bit down on velvet and turned himself so. Or struck a bargain with the coordinates of faith. The walks are no longer singular nor leisurely, this peace that comes through a set stride, falling back into it, a freight of too-soft coal. His entire skin escapes unawares. Then, in an effort to walk never less than singularly, he disguises himself as his own companion and inadvertently succeeds. It is the companion that is third; invents a century. Permission to sing. A ball of light propelled through the funnel like a ball struck by a pool cue. All the populations remaindered from what I see. A loom. The mixture is of each part presenting itself as having never left, a return of what I thought I had actually lost. A colored strand, an emblem in chemicals. Having planted a ridge of roses as the land between myself and he. The companion of too-soft coal. Is it play? Are those crickets? Stepping in, stepping back . . . what the note wrote in the hand of the body that slid down the wall, lying like a sack at my feet.

MERCURY RISING (A VISUALIZATION)

Mercury: 1300–50; ME *Mercurie* < ML, L *Mercurius*, akin to *merx* goods
—*Webster's College Dictionary*

Q. *Why is not the air in* CITIES *so* FRESH, *as that in the* COUNTRY?
A. Because it is impregnated with the *breath* of its numerous inhabitants . . .
—from *Guide to Science*, 1868 by Rev. Dr. Brewer

1A.

there will be three parts.
pay attention to your breath.
breathe deeply,
in through your nose,
out through your mouth.

feel the breath in your belly and hold it,
then release.

when you breathe out,
your breath becomes visible,
a mist
that you inhale through your nose
and exhale from your mouth
in a circle.

you are surrounded by this mist,
and it becomes denser,
like a fog.

then the fog clears
and you are on the bank of a river.

listen to the sound of the wide river.

look out and see the opposite bank.
there is a sandy beach and a forest beyond the sand.

there is a boat with an old woman and an old man
and without a word
they take you across to the other side.

as they take you, you can see stones,
clear water,
you can hear the water against the sides of the boat.

when you get to the sandy beach
you get out of the boat
knowing that it will be there
for you
when you return
and you leave the boat, the man and woman, behind.

1B.

there will be three parts that lead to others. pay attention to your breath. breathe deeply, in through your nose, out through your mouth. hold it, then release. you are northwest of las vegas. when you breathe out, your breath is a vapor that lifts back up and you inhale it through your nose like a circle. you are 36 million miles from the sun, small and singular. study the explosion clouds of bombs in the height of the cold war. this place is not really a place, just housing. you are on an empty street and the light is bright and hot. no atmosphere to ward off or soften impact. you pass a movie theater, a bowling alley, both now closed. you notice that one side of the street is unbearably hot and the other side has ice in its corners. the eccentric orbit rotates three times for every two revolutions. twenty newspaper boxes. you stop for a moment and listen to the air and it streams around the debris. dust carried by solar wind. hot enough to melt lead. there are voices in the distance and you walk toward them and the fluorescent lights above. a group of VIPs sit on bleachers. they watch the desert floor crater like the moon in the wake of over 900 explosions. where the surface is fractured is called "weird terrain." there are mountains, valleys, ridges. compression folds crisscross the plains. listen to the testing, the houses collapsing under the mushroom vapor, searing the skin of pigs. tidal bulges are raised by the sun. you walk past the shattered structures and mock bridges. on your right is a clearing and you go there. in the clearing is a gun turret once used to measure the atmosphere, now inhabited by birds. you ask the bird a question and it gives you an answer. you walk back into the zone of controlled space. a large iron core provides a magnetic shield against solar storms. there will always be a use for this. you stop at a barrier where you are met by a uniformed guard. there is a gun in his holster. he looks you up and down and then lets you proceed to base camp. the streets are named Buster, Teapot, Crossroad. you walk between the empty office buildings and look up at the sky, then the horizon. you see that the light has changed, and that a little time has passed.

1C.

In the solar system, Mercury is the planet closest to the sun. You can see it in the sky only in the morning and at sunset (in the northern hemisphere, it's close to the horizon). The Greeks initially thought it was two planets and named the morning one Apollo and the sunset one Hermes. But they eventually determined it was in fact one planet, and the Romans renamed it Mercury. The planet has temperatures that range from a high of 800°F to a low of −350°F. It was once thought to be "tidally locked," with one side always facing the sun and one side always in darkness. This theory was debunked in the 1960s, when Mercury was proved to have an eccentric orbit. In 1974 the Mariner spaceship did a flyby and mapped almost half of Mercury's surface. In 2008, the Messenger mapped another 30%.

Mercury, Nevada is located near the Nellis Air Force Range and the Nevada Test Site. Nuclear bombs were tested above ground from 1951–1963, after which testing continued underground until 1992. The explosions in the tunnels formed craters on the desert surface. After 1992, some "subcritical" testing continued in order to "protect the safety of the U.S. nuclear stockpile." No one ever officially lived in Mercury—most of the workers commuted from Las Vegas—but sometimes they stayed overnight in the dormitories, bowled in the bowling alley, ate at the steak house. It's unclear what the site is used for now.

2A.

you take the trail into the forest,
look up at the trees,
the streams of light coming down through the branches.

you walk on a bed of pine needles.

on your left,
a little ways off the path,
you see a clearing where there's a small animal.

you ask the animal a question and it gives you an answer.
"vapor."
you thank it for that and return to the path.

as you walk along
you see something shiny
and when you get closer
you see it's a key.

you pick it up and put it in your pocket.

further along off to the right,
you see another clearing,
and another small animal awaits you.

you ask it a question.

it gives you an answer, but it's hard to make out.
you can sense a word forming with an 'r':
"reality"?
and you thank it for that.

you return to the trail.

2B.

there will be three parts that each split into three parts and those parts will break into others. pay attention to your breath as usual. a circle of vapor moves in through your nose and out through your mouth. a circle of vapor thickens into a fog and for a moment you cannot see. inhale the heavy water. crystal shards of terrigen mist allow you to move so fast, you can double back on your own timeline. the line is covered in pine needles that soften the sound of your steps. you look up and the sun threads through the trees. two entwined snakes and a lyre from a tortoise shell to steal and sell for profit. on your left is a small clearing where a sparrow awaits. you approach the sparrow and ask a question. instead of an answer, you're given an assignment. you must carry a dream from the sparrow to a sleeper cell further in the woods. carry on in swift flight and syncretically combine with all the winged others: helmet, staff, sandals and such—the ones who move toward speed force. you have the power to jump time and populate the forest with temporal dupes. back on the path is a sequence of boundaries for crossing over into Arcadia. there's something shiny up ahead, a key, pick it up. you can mark speed with lines, but multiples are better. off to the right is another clearing, another small animal, perhaps a groundhog running back and forth from grass to cairn of stones. you ask it a question. it reveals and interprets. the stones of the cairn are soldered cans of speed. they write a family tree in chalk: grandson of Atlas, son of Zeus, father of Pan, godfather of Barry Allen and all of his ilk. you thank it for that and return to the trail, but the trail begins to split unmarked. you sense someone behind you. but when you turn around, there is only hum, vibration, and spin. pay attention to your breath, don't panic. you look up at the sun and bathe in its chemicals. close your eyes and listen. now open your eyes. see that there are two worlds, gold and silver, and you can run between the two of them on a thread of snow.

2C.

Hermes was the Greek god of boundaries, travelers, shepherds, thieves, poets, commerce, etc. He was pretty much the intermediary for any kind of exchange, transition, or crossing over—thus his role as psychopomp, leading Eurydice back to the underworld after Orpheus gave in to his fears and stole a glance. The Romans adapted him as Mercury and kept him in the same outfit: winged hat, winged sandals, winged staff. Julius Caesar remarked that Mercury was a popular god with conquered populations; they often melded his attributes with gods of their own.

The Flash was created for DC Comics in 1940 and he had numerous incarnations. The first—the Golden Age Flash—was Jay Garrick, a college student who after inhaling heavy water vapors, gained incredible speed. In public his body would vibrate so fast that his face was always blurred and no one could ever identify him. The second—the Silver Age Flash—was police scientist Barry Allen, who enjoyed reading comics about the Golden Age Flash. One day in the lab a bolt of lightning hit and he was bathed in chemicals which gave him great speed. In an homage to the first Flash, he donned a similar outfit and purpose. Eventually, he discovered that he could move so fast that he could jump time; his power became temporal. While time-traveling in the past he met the Golden Age Flash and they became fast friends. They used their time-jumping abilities to cross over into their parallel worlds. Neither Flash should be confused with the somewhat more poignant Pietro Django Maximoff, a.k.a. Quicksilver, depressed and addicted to the crystal shards of terrigen mist that jut from his chest.

3A.

soon you see that you're coming to the center of the forest
and there's a wide clearing with a house there.

it's your house
and it's exactly the kind of house in which you would most like
to live.

you take out the key and open the door.

you can close and lock it behind you if that makes you
feel safer.

you know that your favorite room is in the basement.
you find the stairway and begin to go down:
first step, second step, third.

when you get to the bottom,
you know which door opens to your favorite room
and you go in there.

in that room is exactly what you would want in a room:
the kind of light, the temperature, everything is what you want.

in the corner is a comfortable couch.
you lie down on it and ask yourself what are your goals,
what do you hope to accomplish and create.

and you know the answers.

eventually, you get up from the couch, out of the room, and
back up the stairs.
first step, second step, third.

you unlock the door, let yourself out, lock the door behind you:
you will be back.

there will be three parts that first appear separate but then form a connection of liquid silver. breathe deeply. in through the nose, out the mouth, release your metal breath into the air. control your emissions within the limits of law. the power plant incinerates coal and gold in particulate mist that is your breath. the volcanoes spike the atmosphere. you've come to a house of exploded debris, an emperor's tomb; he died from the pills of eternal life. your breath is carried by wind and mixes with snow, rain, dust. in your hand is a key and you unlock the door and step down into the depths. there is light streaming, a connective world with multiple paths. your breath alloys with silver, gold and tin—but not iron. so you trade your exhalations in an iron flask for a reduction of mineral cinnabar. the room is exactly as you like it: a comfortable couch in the corner, rotating liquid on a disk that silvers the mirrors, arc rectifiers. the snow, rain, and dust layer the lakes and streams and sink with your aspirations. you think about your goals and take the jump test to check your weight. the fish absorb and swim away from the lure. you measure the temperature with thermometers, barometers, thermostats. a spider bites your silver skin. you ask yourself if you are safe in an inoculation of light. the sparrow eats the spider. listen carefully. you can hear the illegal miners refining gold and silver ore. and their fishing lures: violent poison. cumulative poison. separating the fur from the pelt. the fish return your breath as liquid silver. look at yourself in the mirror. you get up and leave the room, lock the door behind you. first the tremors in the hands, then eyelids, lips, and tongue. you take the path back into the forest and walk toward the river. vivid dreams delivered, restless sleep. you pass the clearing, now on your left, but the animal is no longer there. memory loss. you send your thanks to it anyway. cough. you pass the other clearing, now on your right, and although the animal is no longer there, you send it your thanks. psychotic reactions, delirium, hallucinations. when you emerge from the forest you look up at the sky and you can see that the light has changed and a little bit of time has passed.

3C.

The chemical symbol for mercury is Hg, which stands for "hydrargyrum"—the Latinized Greek for "liquid silver." It's named after the Roman god Mercury, perhaps because of its liquid state—it won't stabilize into fixed form unless its 39 degrees below zero. It runs amok. At 680 degrees, it rises in fumes. The metal was once thought to prolong life: China's first emperor went insane and died from mercury pills that he hoped would make him immortal. Mercury alloys easily with silver, tin and gold, and is often used to extract those metals from mines. But it doesn't amalgamate with iron, so an iron flask is considered safe storage. Although it's incredibly poisonous, mercury is easy to find everywhere. It's used in barometers to ascertain the weight of the atmosphere. It's used in mascara. It's also extensively used in medicine and can be found in antiseptics, antidepressants, and vaccines. When my father was just starting out as a chemist, he and his lab partners would take the mercury jump test. They marked the height of their jumps the way a parent marks the height of a growing child. If in future days you can't make the jump, it means the mercury is weighing you down. It was a heavy metal joke.

Half of the mercury in our atmosphere comes from volcanic eruptions (when Krakatoa blew its top in 1883, there was a giant spike in atmospheric mercury levels around the globe). The other half of the mercury in our air is produced primarily by power plants (particularly those that combust coal), hazardous waste incineration, and gold mining. Once the element enters the air, it falls down eventually, coating the leaves of trees and mixing with our water sources. Spiders and small fish absorb the metal easily, and these feeder creatures are then eaten by birds and larger fish. Mercury doesn't dissipate in its toxicity; rather it accumulates greater power as it works its way up the food chain. It goes in through the nose and out the mouth in a circle. When you get back to the river bank, the old woman and old man are waiting for you in their boat and they take you back across. You can see the fish in the water, and gold-colored stones. When you reach the other side you get out of the boat. You close your eyes and take a deep silver breath. You very slowly open your eyes and you are here, in this room, with the light as it is.

POPULAR SCIENCE

"Precise experiment and exact measurement," wrote Marey, "have begun to appear even in the phenomena of thought." I discuss this chronometric experimentation to show that the science of data collection was beginning to affect the cerebral. The darkness shrank before science.

—Francois Dagognet, *Étienne-Jules Marey : A Passion for the Trace*

. . . instead of revealing the beautiful complexity at our core, we live in a culture where dull biological platitudes make headlines and irritating scientific clichés win arguments. In response, we do not need a simpler culture but one that embraces complexity.

—Vaughan Bell, "Our Brains and How They're Not As Simple as We Think"

If you look at the PET scan, I look just like one of those killers.

—James Fallon on "Morning Edition," NPR

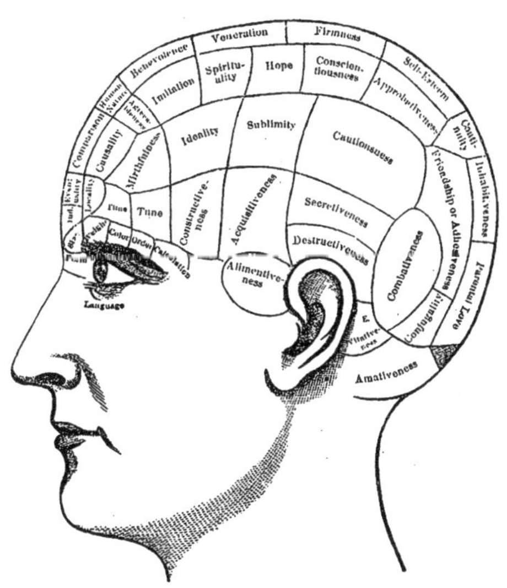

Not long ago, about the closing in of an evening in autumn, I searched and scrolled near the large bay window of D— Coffee-House in Philadelphia and happened upon an interesting literary footnote: In 1849, six years prior to the first edition of *Leaves of Grass*, Walt Whitman visited the Phrenological Cabinet of Fowler & Wells to get his head examined.

the pulses of your brain await their chance

Phrenology—the science of discerning one's character by mapping and measuring the shape of the skull—first appeared in 1796, with the research of a German neuroanatomist named Franz Joseph Gall, who went on to publish a book called *The Anatomy and Physiology of the Nervous System in General, and of the Brain in Particular, with Observations upon the possibility of ascertaining the several intellectual and moral dispositions of man and animal by the configuration of their Heads*.

According to Gall's system, each hill and groove on the surface of the skull represents the location of specific mental faculties beneath; a person could be known simply through intent observation and gentle prodding of the cranium. In 1832 Gall's collaborator, J.G. Spurzheim, introduced phrenology to the United States, where it was popularized by brothers Lorenzo and Orson Fowler, who were later joined by an associate, Samuel Roberts Wells. With offices in Philadelphia, New York, and Boston, and a publishing arm that produced books, pamphlets, self-help manuals, and journals, Fowler & Wells made phrenology a national sensation. In addition to Whitman, those who presented their skulls for analysis included Margaret Fuller, Oliver Wendell Holmes, Allan Pinkerton, Mark Twain, and Horace Mann.

After poring over advertisements for indispensible handbooks and illustrated "cyclopedias," I peered through the smoky glass into the street. It was getting dark and rush hour was in full swing. I wasn't sure, but I thought I caught a glimpse of a familiar figure in the sidewalk throng, then lost sight of him. I turned back to my work.

they seep between regions
a faint blue veneer

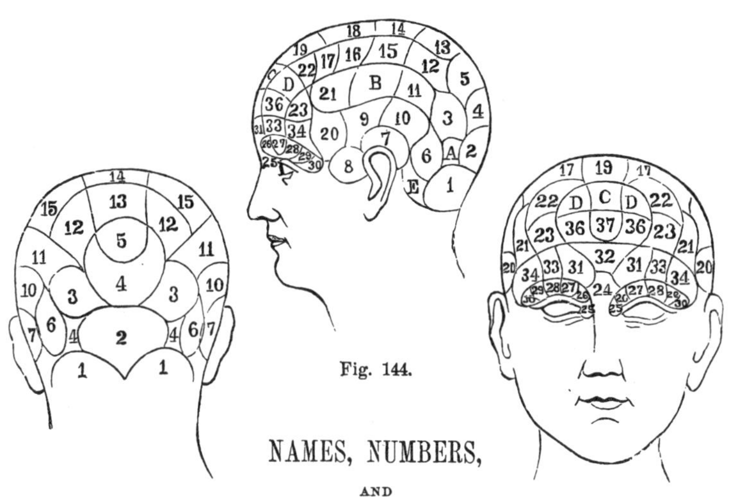

Fig. 144.

NAMES, NUMBERS,

AND

LOCATION OF THE ORGANS.

1. Amativeness.
A. Conjugal Love.
2. Parental Love.
3. Friendship.
4. Inhabitiveness.
5. Continuity.
E. Vitativeness.
6. Combativeness.
7. Destructiveness.
8. Alimentiveness.
9. Acquisitiveness.
10. Secretiveness.
11. Cautiousness.
12. Approbativeness.
13. Self-Esteem.
14. Firmness.
15. Conscientiousness.
16. Hope.
17. Spirituality.
18. Veneration.
19. Benevolence.
20. Constructiveness.
21. Ideality.
B. Sublimity.
22. Imitation.
23. Mirth.
24. Individuality
25. Form.
26. Size.
27. Weight.
28. Color.
29. Order.
30. Calculation.
31. Locality.
32. Eventuality,
33. Time.
34. Tune.
35. Language.
36. Causality.
37. Comparison.
C. Human Nature.
D. Suavity.

Whitman submitted his skull for review by the Fowlers more than once (the first report concluded that Whitman "by practice might make a good accountant"). He reprinted his favorite phrenological summary five times—once in an anonymous review of his own work. The tenets of phrenology happily confirmed his self-concept:

> Leading traits of character appear to be Friendship, Sympathy, Sublimity, and Self Esteem, and markedly among his combinations the dangerous faults of Indolence, a tendency to the pleasures of Voluptuousness and Alimentiveness, and a certain reckless swing of animal will, too unmindful, probably, of the conviction of others.

Although Whitman's love affair with phrenology eventually came to an end as the practice fell out of favor, I found traces of it scattered throughout the drafts and final versions of his poems. "Song of the Broadaxe" (which first appeared in the second edition of *Leaves of Grass*, published by Fowler & Wells in 1856) celebrates the individualized "shapes of America" as well as the faculties listed in Whitman's phrenological chart:

> Never offering others, always offering himself,
> corroborating his phrenology,
> Voluptuous, inhabitive, combative, conscientious,
> alimentive, intuitive, of copious friendship, sublimity,
> firmness, self-esteem, comparison, individuality, form,
> locality, eventuality,
> Avowing by life, manners, works, to contribute
> illustrations of results of The States . . .

The poems "Faces," "Mediums," and "By Blue Ontario's Shore" also make use of phrenology's terms.

> "My brain, it shall be your occult convolutions"
> "To feed the greed of the belly the brain is liberally
> spooning"
> "All beauty comes from beautiful blood and a
> beautiful brain"
> "The pulses of your brain waiting their chance"

1

Phrenological Description of W. (Age 29 Occupation Printer) Whitman by L. N. Fowler N. York July 16 – 1849.

You were blessed by nature with a good constitution and power to live to a good old age. You were undoubtedly descended from a long-lived family. You were not (like many) prematurely developed – did not get ripe like a hothouse plant but you can last long and grow better as you grow older if you are careful to obey the laws of health of life and of mental and physical developement.

"[you] did not get ripe like a hothouse plant but you can last long and grow better": from Walt Whitman's first phrenological report, written by Lorenzo Fowler, 1849.

Eventually I left D— Coffee-House and joined the waver, jostle and hum. Navigating the narrow city sidewalks, we moved in coordinated relation, a sea of human heads. Although I knew not my fellow passengers, I recognized their types: businessmen, administrative assistants, med students, working mothers, etc. And then, up ahead—could it be?—the familiar figure. I pushed through the crowd in his direction, but he had already disappeared.

the pulses swarm, flock, shoal

Weeks later, passing time at an airport newsstand, I noticed several magazines with cover stories on the brain: *Time* had a cartoonish image riffing on Spurzheim's diagram with a headline announcing the "Science of Optimism: Hope isn't rational—so why are humans wired for it?" *Scientific American Mind* featured a story about the "weird" brains of creative people. *Psychology Today*'s main story, "Clues to Character," listed a set of "stable traits" that help predict behavior; knowing these traits could help you find a partner or evaluate a job candidate. The soft science of Whitman's day—with its desire to attach character traits to specific regions of the brain—seemed alive and well in the popular press.

In organized formation, several planes arrived in close succession. Suddenly the corridor filled with a swarm of bodies heading toward baggage claim, each looking for the gap that would allow progress forward. I recognized the looks, the tired faces energized by the release onto solid ground. I recognized the purposeful pace and pattern.

The nineteenth-century doctrine of the skull eventually gave way to the twentieth-century doctrine of the neuron, and the sideshow spectacle of phrenology was deemed a pseudo-science. By the twenty-first century, functional magnetic resonance imaging as well as positron emission tomography, electroencephalography, and computerized axial tomography were busy gathering concrete proof of various locational neuronal theories. At least that's the way it seemed, as I read about the areas of the brain lighting up while waiting in the gate area.

We boarded, in an order, a coalition of partners. The plane was packed and we began the negotiation of how to sit so close together and yet maintain our personal space. As we sat facing forward, the plane followed the dotted line of a predetermined trajectory from here to there. First this, then that. When we arrived, we filed off the plane and were released onto solid ground. We were free of each other but continued to move in relation, a system of interacting dynamics.

as crickets sync
they merge and sing in a changing cycle
femurs against forewings

Back at home, a thick humid fog hung over the city, and the streets seemed empty. In the library this time, I continued my research. Could the brain fit inside a single sentence? I turned the pages, hoping for the film from the mental vision to depart, peering through the smoky panes into the street. Thirty-seven mental and moral faculties. Eighty billion neurons with trillions of synaptic connections between them. Centers or systems? Symmetry-making or symmetry-breaking? I was hitting up against a language problem. I looked at the words in their aggregate relations. Until very late at night.

"Leading traits of character appear to be FRIENDSHIP, SYMPATHY, SUBLIMITY, and SELF ESTEEM . . ."

ILLUSTRATION 1: FRIENDSHIP (ALSO CALLED ADHESIVENESS)

3. ADHESIVENESS.

Situated on each side of Concentrativeness, higher up than Philoprogenitiveness, just above the lambdoidal suture. The medial prefrontal cortex signals someone of value. Frontal systems linked with limbic circuits facilitate love of friends. Coping with frenemies. Judgments about the close others increased blood oxygenation level-dependent response along the frontal midline. I have seen boys, also, walk in the street with their arms twined around each other's necks, and always in each other's society. They say they love each other very much. Social closeness is the primary factor, rather than shared beliefs, as previously assumed. It is right, children, to exercise this organ. Regions that respond to information about friends are shown in orange; regions that respond more to strangers are in blue. While in the scanner they played "The Newlywed Game": would a friend or stranger prefer an aisle or window seat? Sheep skip and play together in the open field. This is true of almost all animals, and they, with us, have a little prominence on their skulls, caused by the development of the brain, which we call Adhesiveness. Sure enough, the bigger the amygdala, the larger and more complex a person's social network tended to be. Mlle. N. "was so tenderly attached to a lady of her own age, that neither marriage nor the solicitations of her mother could induce her to leave her." This finding is exciting because it opens a window into exploring abnormalities in the amygdala. The organ is large in Mrs. H. and Mary Macinnes—Established. For more on

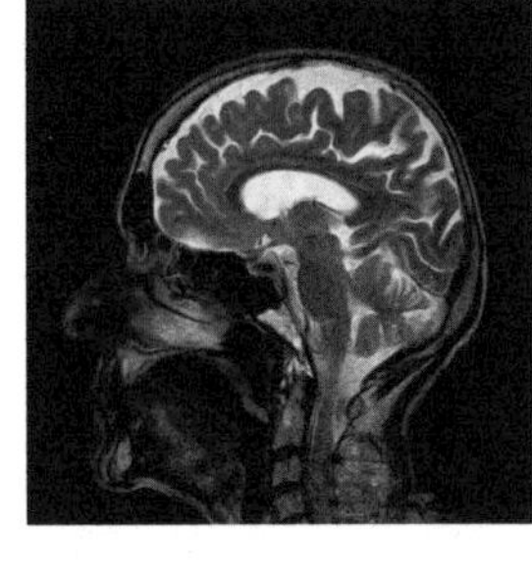

how experience changes the brain, check out my new book.

George Combe, *Elements of Phrenology*; "Brain responds more to close friends, imaging study shows," *Science Daily*; Krienen, Tu, and Buckner, "Clan Mentality: Evidence that Medial Prefrontal Cortex Responds to Close Others," *Journal of Neuroscience*; Kirsten Weir, "Fickle Friends: How to Deal with Frenemies," *Scientific American Mind*; Lydia Folger Fowler, *Familiar Lessons on Phrenology: Designed for the Use of Children and Youth*; Susan Weinschenk, "100 Things You Should Know About People: #88—Your Brain Has A Special Response to People You Know, *The Team W Blog*; Jeanna Bryner, "Brains Hard-Wired to Connect with Friends," *LiveScience.com*; Sian Beilock, "When It Come to Our Social Networks, Brain Size Matters," *Psychology Today*; Samuel Roberts Wells, *How to Read Character: A New Illustrated Hand-book of Phrenology*.

In 1849 (the same year as Whitman's first phrenological exam), in an article published in the *American Phrenological Journal*, the Fowler brothers wrote "Our present desire is this—TO PHRENOLOGIZE OUR NATION, for thereby it will REFORM THE WORLD." 1849 was also the year when the United States Department of the Interior was established. Manifest destiny was in full force.

FIG. 118.—ARTEMUS WARD.* FIG. 119.—KANOSH, AN INDIAN CHIEF.

According to Samuel Wells in *How to Read Character*, "the organ of Mirthfulness is situated on the side of the upper part of the forehead." The illustration above was presented as proof, with a footnote stating "Mr. Charles F. Brown, better known as 'Artemus Ward,' was one of the most noted of American humorists. Mirthfulness is seen to be very well developed. The contrast between his head and that of the Indian Chief is very striking." In phrenology, bigger was always better. If an organ area was found to be "small," the Fowlers provided tips on how to exercise the region so as to promote its growth. The brain, like the body, was a muscle to be worked. If the Indian Chief wished to enlarge that portion of his brain associated with mirth, he was advised:

> The facetious aspects of things and subjects should be contemplated, and the idea that dignity and self-respect require perpetual seriousness must be resolutely combated. The company of mirthful people should be sought, for nothing is more contagious than genuine jollity. There is a time to laugh as well as a time to weep, and laughter is

promotive of health and longevity. The injunction to "laugh and grow fat!" is not without a physiological reason, nor is the Shaksperian adage that "a light heart lives long," a mere poetical flourish.

But of course this instruction wasn't meant for the Indian Chief.

aggregate choruses
temporary unisons that then move on

Mark Twain had his skull read several times by Lorenzo Fowler; the first time he used an assumed name, and the phrenological report revealed a cavity that "represented a total absence of the sense of humor." When he returned for a second reading a few months later (this time with a calling card stating his real name as well as his pen name), the cavity suddenly transformed into a lofty bump of mirthfulness. He wrote of his visits to Fowler: "These experiences have given me a prejudice against phrenology which has lasted until now. I am aware that the prejudice should have been against Fowler, instead of against the art—But, I am human, and that is not the way prejudices act."

The frontal lobe is the only part of the brain where a phrenological mapping coincides with a contemporary assignment of functional location: the faculty of "mirthfulness" is said to be exactly where the left prefrontal cortex lights up on fMRI scans when people are happy.

a glacier of fluids,
the coincidence of their calls

ILLUSTRATION 2: SYMPATHY (ALSO CALLED BENEVOLENCE)

Directly in front of Veneration is a piece of brain that induces us to be kind hearted. Some people lack those feelings and may behave in anti-social ways that can be extremely costly to society. Oxytocin is known as the "love hormone" because it encourages trust, cooperation and social bonding. Suppressed when the story content and expression were mismatched; having a person smile while telling about his mother's death. You *can* restrain excesses, and *can* cultivate deficiencies. You may be intellectual, you may be social, but the *moral* nature is the *"crown of glory,"* and nothing can atone for the absence of it, or supply its place. Activation in the ventromedial prefrontal cortex and superior frontal gyrus, regions that deal with social conflict. Men have more of this working Benevolence than women, and it is proper they should have, as their power to help is greater; but women are more sympathetic and more readily touched by pity. Murderers generally have the forehead "villainously low" in the region of Benevolence. People with low activity in the orbital cortex are either free-wheeling types or sociopaths. When Destructiveness is large and this organ small, cruelty may result. Dutch men who inhaled oxytocin were more likely to associate positive words, such as joy and laughter, and complex positive emotions, such as hope and admiration, with Dutch people than with Germans or Arabs. It has been objected that Nature cannot have placed a faculty of Benevolence, and another of Destructiveness, in the same mind; but

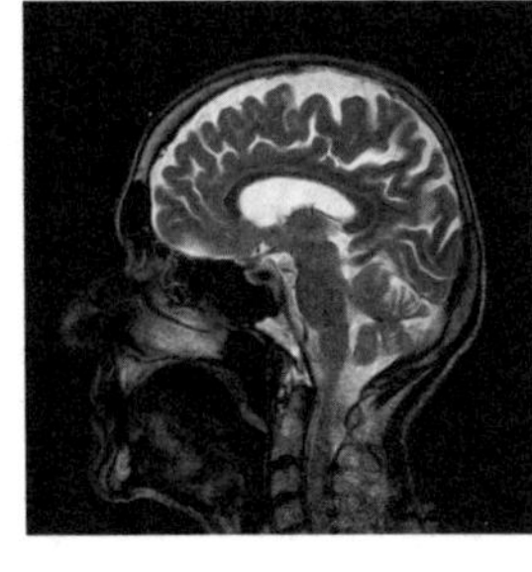

Man is confessedly an assemblage of contradictions. All can improve if they have the desire; restrain your feelings that that organ will increase in size; the brain will enlarge, and will press out the skull. A very basic way we connect to other people.

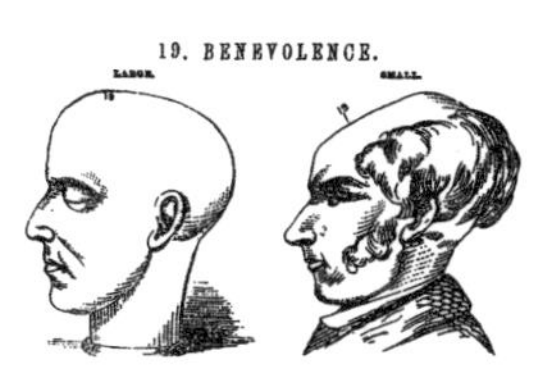

Lydia Folger Fowler, *Familiar Lessons on Phrenology: Designed for the Use of Children and Youth*; "Search for Sympathy Uncovers Patterns of Brain Activity," *Science Daily*; Janelle Weaver, "The Prejudice Hormone: Oxytocin, Known for Encouraging Bonding, May Underlie Bias," *Scientific American Mind*; Clara Moskowitz, "Neuroscience May Explain the Dalai Lama," *NBCNews.com*; Samuel Roberts Wells, *How to Read Character: A New Illustrated Hand-book of Phrenology*; Barbara Bradley Hagerty, "A Neuroscientist Uncovers A Dark Secret, *NPR*; George Combe, *Elements of Phrenology*.

According to the tenets of phrenology, interior traits are legible, an open territory to be read and analyzed. The head is a map of self-help; all flaws can be conquered, rewritten, perfected. As Walt Whitman wrote in response to first hearing a lecture by Orson Fowler, "If the professor can, as he professes, teach men to know their intellectual and moral deficiencies and remedy them, we do not see that our people may long remain imperfect."

"Our people" was a category limited to those with white skin; it was the white person who could benefit from the brain's flexibility and all others were stuck with an array of imperfect presets. Thus, the discourse of phrenology attached itself to a long history of discriminatory nationalisms and racist essentialisms:

> The special organs in which the Caucasian brain most excels, and which distinguish it from those of all less advanced races, are Mirthfulness, Ideality, and Conscientiousness, the organs of these faculties being almost invariably small in savage and barbarous tribes. (Wells, vii)

> The breadth of the wings of the nose next to the face indicates Secretiveness. This is in accordance with the physiological action of this faculty which tends to shut the mouth and expand the nostrils. This sign is large in the Negro, the Chinese, the North American Indian and in most savage and half-civilized tribes. (Wells, 63)

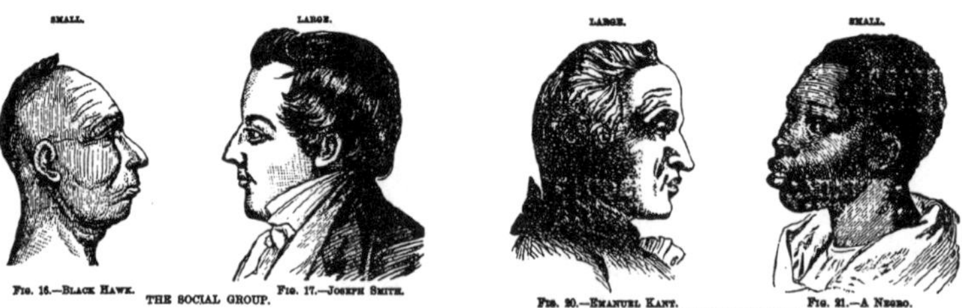

Fig. 16.—Black Hawk. THE SOCIAL GROUP. Fig. 17.—Joseph Smith.

Fig. 20.—Emanuel Kant. REFLECTIVE GROUP. Fig. 21.—A Negro.

Today, it is proposed that if the rationalism of the pre-frontal cortex could suppress the emotionality produced by the amygdala and the ventral striatum, perhaps racism could be prevented. Newsstand magazines and digital clickbait tell us the prefrontal cortex is our best hope. There was the neuroscientist who had a number of murderers in his family tree. Upon reviewing his own brain scan, he discovered that his orbital cortex—the area of the brain thought to control ethical behavior and impulse control—was inactive. He wondered, might he be a psychopath-in-waiting? For the phrenologists, the link of location to behavior provided a seductive narrative structure of legible cause and effect. If this, then that. In the article about the neuroscientist, I sensed the allure of that structure still simmering.

B. SUBLIMITY.

Situated on the side-head, directly above Acquisitiveness and behind Ideality, the doughnut-shaped machine swallows the nun. A high-tech attempt to read her mind as she communes with her deity. The vast, the grand, the majestic: Is there a God spot in the brain? Pin down what happens in the brain when people experience mystical awakenings. One with large Sublimity would enjoy scenery similar to that represented in the cut. When the Buddhists lost their sense of existence as separate individuals, the researchers injected them with a radioactive isotope that is carried by the blood to active brain areas. It is designed to represent the waters rushing and tumbling over the rocks at the Falls of Niagara. A large drop in activity in a portion of the parietal lobe, which encompasses the back of the brain, and an increase in activity in the right prefrontal cortex, which resides behind the forehead. They love the cragged precipice, the snow-capped mountain, the raging cataract, the burning volcano. Because the affected part of of the parietal lobe normally aids with navigation and spatial orientation, the neuroscientists surmise that its abnormal silence during meditation underlies the perceived dissolution of physical boundaries and the feeling of being at one with the universe. Some would like to sail on the mighty ocean when the angry waves and billows rise around their tempest-tossed ship. fMRI scans of several hundred Buddhist brains from around the world. Sublimity enables us to appreciate mountain scenery, the vastness of the ocean, the grandeur of a thunder-storm,

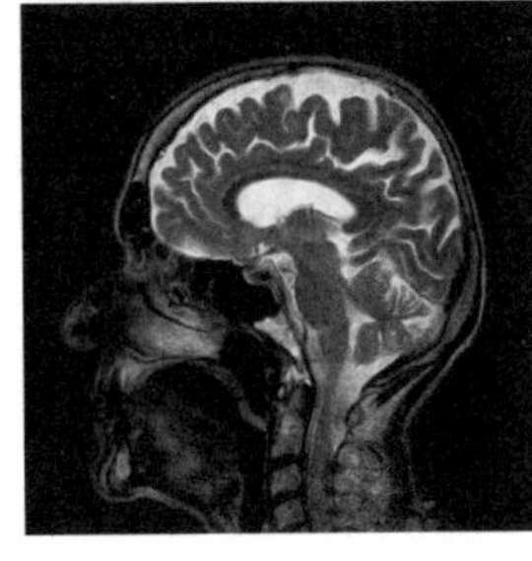

the roar of artillery, the clash of armies, etc. It is possible that some people's brains will simply resist succumbing to the divine. Nature deficit disorder.

Samuel Roberts Wells, *How to Read Character: A New Illustrated Hand-book of Phrenology*; David Biello, "Searching for God in the Brain," *Scientific American Mind*; Ian Sample, " 'God spot' researchers see the light in MRI study," *The Guardian*; Matt Danzico, "Brains of Buddhist Monks scanned in Meditation Study," *BBC News*; Lydia Folger Fowler, *Familiar Lessons on Phrenology: Designed for the Use of Children and Youth*.

as bodies of starlings in cloudstorm form, splay, and re-form

In 1838, Orson Fowler opened a Philadelphia office with his brother-in-law at 210 Chestnut Street. According to Madeleine Stern, in her book *Heads & Headlines: The Phrenological Fowlers*, this "phrenological museum," contained the "rarest assemblage, perhaps, on this continent of unique skulls, and casts of persons now living . . . nearly, if not wholly, unparalleled in the series of cranioscopal formations." Fowler began to publish *The American Phrenological Journal and Miscellany*, which almost instantly plunged his practice into financial ruin. The office closed in 1842; however a new office and bookstore opened in 1854 (this time in partnership with Samuel Wells) at 231 Arch Street.

I decided to visit the sites of these former offices. The United States Custom House (built during the Depression) occupied the location of Orson Fowler's first office. On what I believed to be the site of the second office was a red brick building, with the name "Berger Brothers Company" just barely visible above the first floor. Berger Brothers was a supplier for tinners and roofers in the 1920s.

After mapping these coordinates, I learned that all of the street numbers in Philadelphia were changed in 1857 and my conclusions regarding the sites of the phrenological offices were entirely misinformed. I had tried to understand historical events through location, driven by the belief that if I could see the architectural skeleton, the ghosts of intrinsic structure, perhaps I could understand what had happened at a moment in time. I had placed my hopes on a stabilized regional genealogy, on the pleasures of equating that with this.

pulled together by the simplest of rules:
don't get too close,
don't get too far from your neighbor

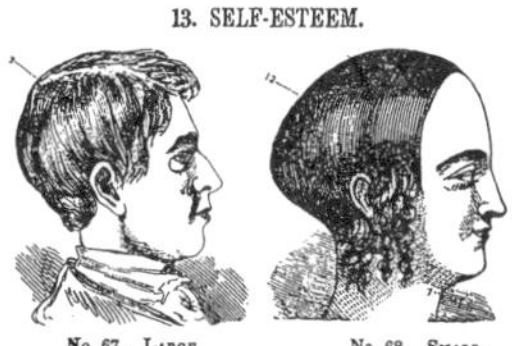

Situated at the vertex of the top-head, where the coronal surface begins to decline. She called on God on every occasion, as if he took a special interest in her affairs. The drive system can turn to the system that will give it a proverbial spanking or the system that will give it a hug. We may attack ourselves. Children with this organ large, think they can do as much as their parents; and often feel as though they were too old to render obedience to their requests, running on oxytocin and intrinsic opiates. Someone is always the head, the captain, or the ruling spirit, and all the others do as he dictates. This makes sense to me from the sociometer perspective. The imposter phenomenon. One man always rules, and another serves; one man makes the laws of the nation, and another obeys them. If a person speaks to another at all disrespectfully, the latter feels that he must challenge him to fight a duel, and endeavor to take his life. Anatomy-based diffusion tensor imaging. Sometimes the organ is too large, and gives a haughty domineering spirit, as is manifested in the cut. She spreads out her beautiful feathers. He saw his violent clients as egotists with a grandiose sense of personal superiority and entitlement. There are persons who are exceedingly censorious, whose conversation is habitually directed to their neighbours' faults, who feel sore when others are elevated, and experience great pleasure in bringing them down. Many schools have students make lists of reasons why they are wonderful people or sing songs of self-celebration. Children in hooting and

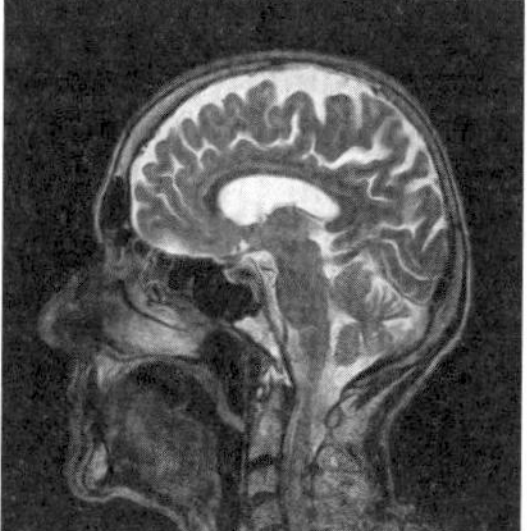

pelting an idiot. Positively correlated with the degree of self-reported social distress experienced during a game of cyberball. Their chief motive is a strong sense of their own superiority. She held her head high and a little backwards. Your brain maintains complex maps for the "pecking order" of the people surrounding you. Self-Esteem corresponds in some measure to the Desire of Power of the metaphysicians. They could see an avatar. It disposes to the use of the *emphatic I* in writing and conversation. "I am a man," Black Hawk said to Jackson. Changes in pecking order brings about changes in how millions of neurons are connected. When the organ becomes excited by disease, the individual is prone to imagine himself a king, emperor, or a transcendent genius, and some have even fancied themselves the Supreme Being. The organ is large in Haggart, the Hindoos, Dempsey; moderate in Dr. Hette, and the American Indians.—Established. Cross-lagged analysis. With more dopamine and other "happy" neurochemicals, an increase in status increases the number of new connections made per hour in the brain.

Fig.10.—Self-Esteem.

Samuel Roberts Wells, *How to Read Character: A New Illustrated Hand-book of Phrenology*; George Combe, *Elements of Phrenology*; Robin Nixon, "The Neuroscience of Self-Esteem, Self-Criticism and Self-Compassion," *LiveScience.com*; Lydia Folger Fowler, *Familiar Lessons on Phrenology: Designed for the Use of Children and Youth*; Roy F. Baumeister, "Violent Pride," *Scientific American Mind*; Keiichi Onoda et. al., "Does low self-esteem enhance social pain?" *Social Cognitive and Affective Neuroscience*; David Rock "Has Coddling an Entire Generation of Children Set Them Up for Failure?" *Psychology Today*.

everyday agents sufficiently stirred by the earth's rotation

In his essay, "Nature," Emerson wrote, "Parts of speech are metaphors because the whole of nature is a metaphor of the human mind." And as nature changes, so do the metaphors. For instance: Hemispheres. Water systems, dams, plumbing. A city, a village. A lost sailor catches a faint glimpse of a lighthouse. A sailor jumps for joy. Cortex bark. Dendrite trees. A piano with a limited number of keys producing an unlimited number of melodies. A steam engine. A railway switching system. A telegraph relays as neurons. An automated factory. A telephone exchange; behavior like a phone call patched through. A train routed to the right track. An adding machine. A library machine. A mechanical calculator. A part going down the assembly line. Crowding problems, traffic jams. A noisy stadium. Lock and key. Photograph as memory. An enchanted loom "where millions of flashing shuttles weave a dissolving pattern." Hydraulic automatons. Nerves are pipes in the system. Croquet. Oscillators. Marbles. Gyroscopes. A Swiss Army knife. A nerve breathes. Wires. The synapse valve. A piano playing a song expressed in cortical vibrations generating thoughts. Gunpowder burning its way down the axon. Diodes, triodes, multi-vibrators. A synapse as resistor, a rheostat. Hardware. Software. Coupled oscillators. Brain as amplifier. A holograph. A computer. A small world network. Parts light up.

wandering stars, confined to no orbit

SELFISH PROPENSITIES.

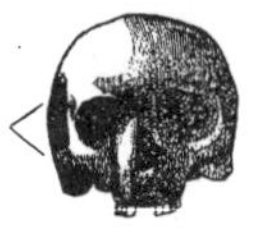

No. 53. Large.

No. 54. Small.

Below and in front of Alimentiveness, we find the region of Relaxation. The pre-motor cortex tends to light up. The lymphatick, or phlegmatick, levels of dopamine. The machine tracked the flow of oxygenated blood, indicated by soft and abundant flesh, and languor of the pulse. A dull, ease-seeking, inefficient temperament could be more about biology than attitude. If a heated atmosphere had been best for man, Nature would have heated it; but it relaxes. The result is a rollercoaster of hippocampal activity depending on the street network. Unless you would make stupid blockheads of your children, do not keep them shut up in a hot-stove room. Distinctions between brains of the apathetic vs. go-getters. A flattened crown indicates a want of ambition, energy, and aspiration. Navigating with GPS is making our brains lazy. Breathe abundantly so as to turn up the surplus carbon; sit little, but walk much. A treatment for those pathological conditions of extreme apathy.

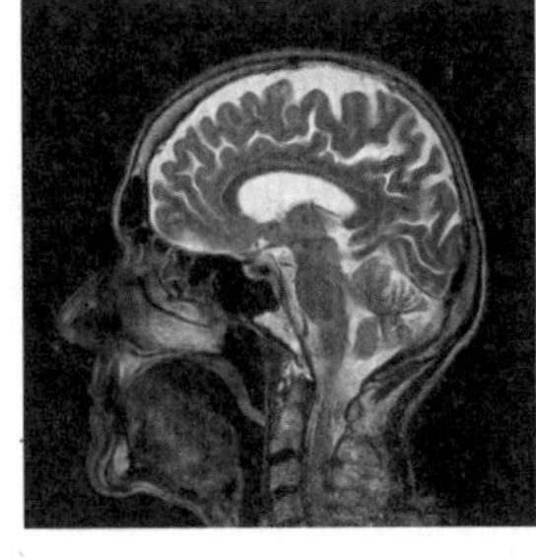

Joseph Rhodes Buchanan, *Buchanan's Journal of Man*; Robert Roy Britt, "Laziness: Blame it on the Brain?" *LiveScience*; Orson Squire Fowler, *Fowler's Practical Phrenology*; Rob Verger, "Navigating with GPS is Making Our Brains Lazy," *Popular Science*; Orson Squire Fowler, *Science of Life: Its Principles, Faculties, Organs, Temperaments*; Orson Squire Fowler, *The Practical Phrenologist*.

a pattern imposed on flow a swarm of small causes in the tent city of neurons

The language of cure is the language of knowing where you are on the map. A bump on the head, a signal of electrical activity, moving down the line from fault to perfection, a localized equivalency. This is the physical script of the modular mind, the narrative arc of see-then-solve. The dream of clean borders and limited cross-overs. The perpetual re-searching for cause and explanation. The desire for a leader, a general, a man at the top.

In opposition, a familiar figure wanders in convolutions, merging with a crowd just leaving a stadium. He moves in response to all the other moves, changing and shifting in relation. A collaboration of parts leading to some form, wired for reciprocity, a response and in turn a stimulus. In other words, a conversation, changing and shifting in circumstance. Everyone finds their way home.

As patterns of being web forward in integrative networks, the defenders of states' rights and strong borders feel the waters rising. They see the regions shifting, dispersing, and they fight for the static quo. Waiting for a small patch of gray matter to light up the night and diagnose the diseases of the mental landscape in a pinpoint.

protesting at the edges of cities, within private parks, beside city halls, on campus lawns

Meanwhile, a figure wandering in convolutions responds with flux, resists the spell of the positron emission, the colorful diagram, the photogenic splice. Behavior colors outside the lines, always on the lam, falling off the map—an unruly region, messing up the works, merging with other processes. Not a mass action, but interactive, spatially responsive, ongoing.

I want to be that figure. Instead I seek the pleasures of neat equations and clean comparisons. My pre-motor cortex lights up. I crave the narrative structure of that equals this. Lazy brain.

ILLUSTRATION 6: VOLUPTUOUSNESS (ALSO CALLED AMATIVENESS)

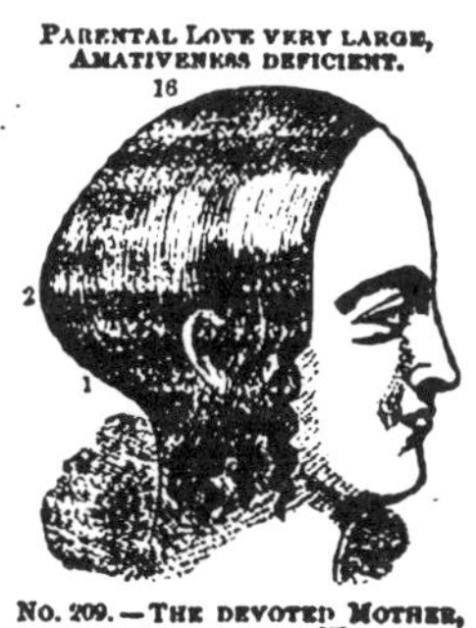

No. 209.—THE DEVOTED MOTHER, BUT INDIFFERENT WIFE.

This organ is located at the back of the head, behind the ears and gives fulness to the neck. A computer-generated map of particularly active areas showed hot spots deep in the brain, below conscious awareness, in areas called the caudate nucleus and the ventral tegmental area, which communicate with each other as part of a circuit. To find it, feel on the middle line toward the base of the skull, at the back part of the head, and you will discover a small bony projection called the occipital process. Close your eyes for a minute and envision all the romantic parts of the human body. Another area that lit up produces dopamine, a powerful neurotransmitter that affects pleasure and motivation. Considerable humidity of the lip. Her front brain is telling her he's trouble, but her middle brain won't listen. Aaron Burr, third Vice-President of the United States, was noted for his debauchery in private life, as well as for his unscrupulous conduct as a statesman. Bet you didn't think about the caudate and the ventral tegmental areas, did you? The men had quite a bit more activity in the brain region that integrates visual stimuli. This isn't surprising considering that men support the porn industry and women spend their lives trying to look good for men. Besotted volunteers in a brain scanner. Any one desiring to cultivate Amativeness, then, should go into society as much as convenient, make it a point to be agreeable as possible to those persons of the other sex. You can almost imagine a time where

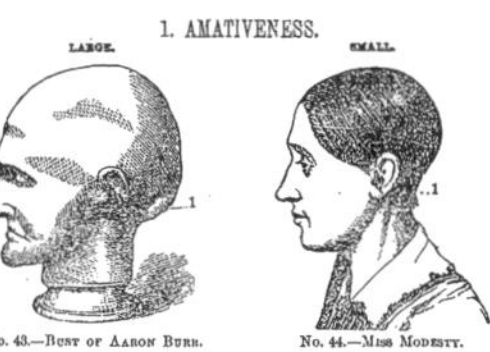

No. 43.—Bust of Aaron Burr. No. 44.—Miss Modesty.

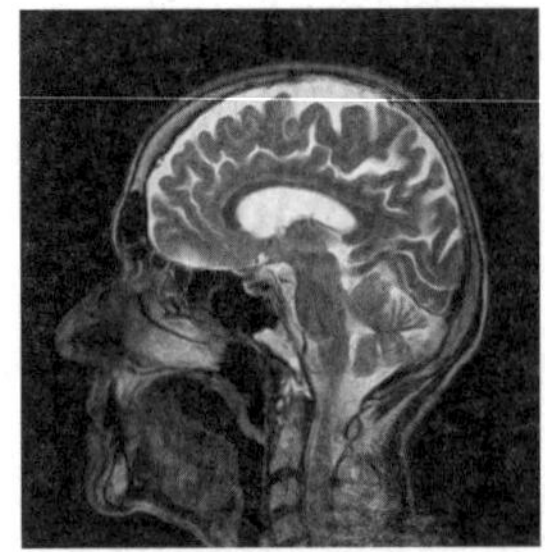

instead of going to Match.com you could have a test to find out whether you're an attachment type or not. If this organ be perverted, or used improperly, it is the means of making men and women very unhappy, and very wicked. Being dumped actually does heighten romantic love, a phenomenon called frustration-attraction. Little blind boy Cupid with a bow and arrow. M.R.I. images, in the caudate nucleus. Excesses are by no means always referable to the organ in the brain. The true cause is often gastric irritation.

Lydia Folger Fowler, *Familiar Lessons on Phrenology: Designed for the Use of Children and Youth*; Benedict Carey, "Watching New Love as It Sears the Brain," *The New York Times*; Samuel Roberts Wells, *How to Read Character: A New Illustrated Hand-book of Phrenology*; Elizabeth Cohen, "Loving with all your . . . brain," *CNN*; "Discovering the Mysteries of Love and the Brain," *Los Angeles Times*; Emily Eakin, "Looking for That Brain Wave Called Love: Humanities Experts Use M.R.I.'s to Scan the Mind for the Locus of the Finer Feelings, *New York Times*.

the pulses travel the same currents

Edgar Allan Poe moved to Philadelphia in the same year Orson Fowler opened his office on Chestnut Street; in fact Poe's publisher worked out of the same building. Although they never met, I imagine Poe and the phrenologists walking the same streets, drinking in the same bars. The result of Poe taking one path while the Fowlers take another creates a circuit in the atmosphere, cells only, pulsing on a matrix of currents.

References to phrenology can be found in a number of Poe's stories (see "Imp of the Perverse," "The Murders in the Rue Morgue," "Ligeia"), but there is no evidence that Poe ever submitted his skull to be analyzed. And though the Fowlers may not have known Poe, they used him (and *not* Walt Whitman) as the embodiment of the "poet's temperament"—nervous and high-strung. After Poe died, the Fowlers released a conjectural phrenological report. His strengths were in the faculties of Ideality, Sublimity, Spirituality, and Language. His weakness was Bibativeness (situated in front of Alimentiveness, near the ears):

> The wine-cup was the bane of his being, and brought out the worst phases of his character; and although his friends claim that this one fault was the procurer of all his waywardness and gained him all his enemies, yet we believe that, artificial excitement aside, he was from the very nature of his organization a wandering star, which could be confined to no orbit and limited to no constellation in the empire of mind.

In my newsfeed I see reports of various stars breaking out of rehab. In *Scientific American Mind*, I find an updated location for bibativeness:

> An alcoholic's problems with social cues are consistent with the "frontal lobe hypothesis," which postulates that damage to the prefrontal cortex—known to be vulnerable to alcohol's toxic effects—leads to behavioral deficits.

constellatory matter repositioning

ILLUSTRATION 7: ALIMENTIVENESS

Regions of the brain linked with pleasurable emotions and sensations—particularly the nucleus accumbens in the ventral striatum. Nearly parallel with the zygomatic arch, exactly under the organ of Acquisitiveness, and before that of Destructiveness. When the teenager was given normal levels of the hormone, brain imaging showed greater activity in the striatum, an area associated with reward. When the organ is large, the head is broad at this part, resulting in an overlapping of flabby integument, which gives a gross animal look to the face. Some appear to have fewer dopamine D2 receptors in key reward regions of the brain than other people—much like drug addicts. Which must not be confounded with high cheek-bones. One should make his table and its belongings as attractive as possible. These brain scans are of an obese teenager whose fat cells were unable to secrete leptin. In the cut, you will see two men very busy with their knives and forks, etc. Thus, it is possible that the relationship between reward neurocircuitry and obesity follows the Goldilocks principle. The perversion of this faculty leads to more misery and unhappiness than almost any other thing. Using fMRI, his team scanned the brains of adolescent girls. The appetite which asks for "Rum, rum." Ratcheted down in our obesogenic world. We may eventually be able to figure out who needs their dopamine cranked up. It exhausts the saliva.

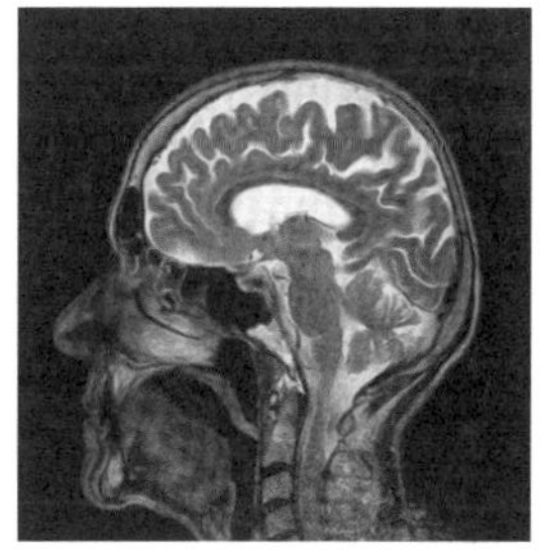

George Combe, *Elements of Phrenology*; Luke Stoeckel, "The Goldilocks Principle or Obesity," *Scientific American Mind*; Samuel Roberts Wells, *How to Read Character: A New Illustrated Hand-book of Phrenology*; J.R. Minkel, "Appetite-Killing Hormone Negates Joy of Eating," *Scientific American Mind*; Lydia Folger Fowler, *Familiar Lessons on Phrenology: Designed for the Use of Children and Youth*.

When I put the maps side by side . . .

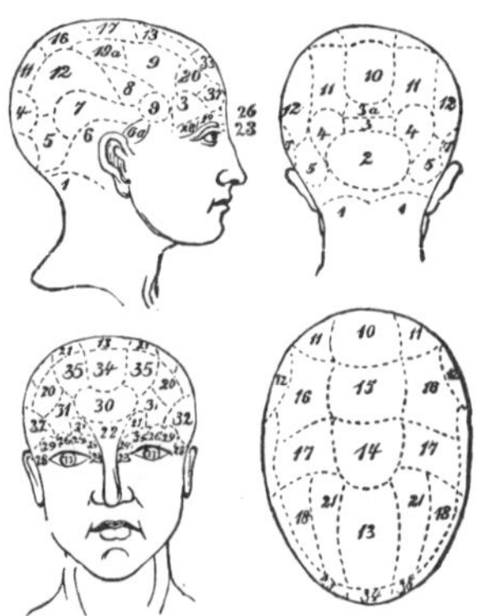

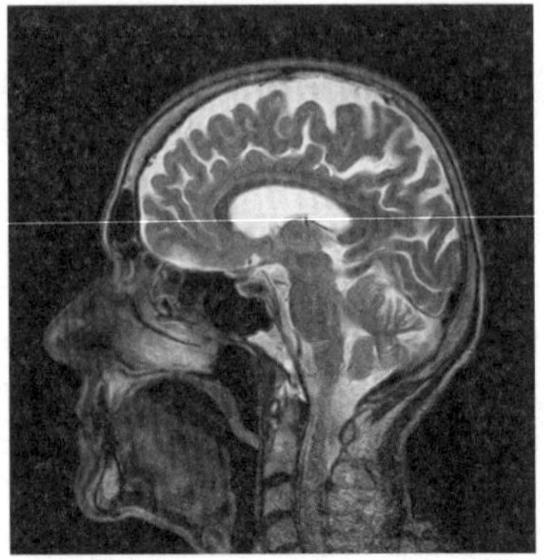

I realize the error of my own thinking, a binary pattern imposed on flow.

A winery matter deposed on dough.

A vine airy scatter reposed on snow.

the smallest interaction can change the states

In Edgar Allan Poe's "The Man of the Crowd," a familiar figure can exist only in the presence of others. Alone on the street, he turns pale, losing his life-blood. When he finds a crowded thoroughfare, "the sounds of human life" revive him. The crowd is the heart, a synergistic system of multifactorial dynamics. I stop fully in front of the wanderer, gaze at him steadfastly in the face.

AN ALTERNATIVE PATTERN

> Letter to the editor of *The New York Times*, 11/14/07, signed by 17 cognitive neuroscientists: " . . . we know that it is not possible to definitively determine whether a person is anxious or feeling connected simply by looking at activity in a particular brain region. This is so because brain regions are typically engaged by many mental states, and thus a one-to-one mapping between a brain region and a mental state is not possible."

Whitman wrote "the pulses of your brain waiting their chance"

they seep between regions and cover the entire cortical surface
with a faint blue veneer

they swarm, flock, shoal

as crickets sync
they merge and sing in a changing cycle
femurs against forewings

aggregate choruses, temporary unisons that then move on
a glacier of fluids,
the coincidence of their calls

the pulses of the brain await their chance
as bodies of starlings in cloudstorm
form, splay, and re-form

pulled together by the simplest of rules:
don't get too close,
don't get too far from your neighbor

everyday agents sufficiently stirred by the earth's rotation
wandering stars, confined to no orbit

a pattern imposed on flow
a swarm of small causes in the tent city of neurons

protesting at the edges of cities, within private parks,
beside city halls, on campus lawns

the pulses travel the same currents
constellatory matter repositioning
the smallest interaction can change “the results of The States.”

SYSTEM OF DISPLAY

The Grooved Brain Coral is named for its appearance. It looks amazingly like a human brain and has particularly deep grooves that resemble the brain's folds. In deeper waters, it can even have a grayish appearance. It is a large, reef-building coral that lives throughout the Caribbean Sea and adjacent waters. The grooves may also resemble a maze or labyrinth, giving rise to the scientific name "labryinthiformis."

—Oceana.org

. . . all nature is so full . . .

—Gilbert White

Wagner Free Institute of Science. Photograph by Joseph Elliott.
Historic American Buildings Survey.

there are general patterns

in this intertidal life

kingdom Animalia

Coral is animal, a colony of polyps dressed in algae. The algae give color, photosynthesizing the sun. Polyps have stingers, graspers, to draw the nutrients in. Then the coral exudes a skeleton, a shelter made from its own interior life.

chora is the dwelling place

life in the marine station

phylum Cnidaria, stinging cells

William Wagner was a cloth merchant's son born in 1796 in Philadelphia. As a child, walking along the Wissahickon creek, he began to collect minerals. Collecting is the first step towards naming.

the outermost layer of the earth curls over & lifts towards the water's surface

look up through the water to the sky

class Anthozoa, flower animals

I might want to make a form that mirrors the coral's reliance on its environment. The polyps are mouths that share their homes with the algae; in exchange the algae produce food that the polyps eat. Except the polyps can't build a home to share without the food in the first place. Sharing simultaneous with just existing.

coral islands circle in the middle of the deep sea

craggy and jeweled before you

order Scleractinia, stony skeleton

Wagner wanted to be a scientist or a doctor, but his father had more lucrative plans for him. He was apprenticed to Stephen Girard, a merchant and banker, and one of the wealthiest men in the entirety of United States history. At twenty-one, Wagner was assigned the job of "supercargo," supervising sales on and off Girard's ship, the *Helvetius*; his older brother, Samuel, was aboard the ship *Rousseau*.

up from the outermost layer at particular sea level

you are just above and just below

family Faviidae or Mussidae, spheres with grooved surfaces

The polyps secrete limestone structures—corallum—that are as solid as walls, as intricate as cities. Reefs might seem an architecture built up from the sea floor, but their existence depends on the ceiling of the sea. We reach for the surface on the backs of our calcified dead. The nineteenth-century geologist Charles Lyell wrote in a letter, "Coral islands are the last efforts of drowning continents to lift their heads above water."

seeming a piece of land, but in fact a team of organisms

read them as evidence, the tip of the iceberg

genus Diploria once Madrepora, doubling back, inlet folds

The ship *Helvetius* was named after the French philosopher Claude Adrien Helvétius. In his book *De L'Esprit* (*Essays On the Mind*), he argued that all inequalities can be traced back to unequal educational opportunities. "I am convinced that a good education would diffuse light, virtue, and consequently, happiness in society; and that the opinion, that genius and virtue are merely gifts of nature, is a great obstacle to the making any farther progress in the science of education . . . " In 1818, the same year William Wagner sailed on the *Helvetius*, the First School District of Pennsylvania was established.

look for proof that something happened here

a gentleman naturalist keeps a weather journal, for instance

species cerebriformis, or brain stone

At night the polyps expand from their cells and hollows. Atoms of living jelly. I might want to make a form with tentacula that protrude and retract as if seizing and devouring. A myriad of offensive weapons contained in capsules, in a world of potential enemies. In a letter to his sister in 1834, Charles Darwin wrote "I have lately determined to work chiefly amongst the Zoophites or Coralls: it is an enormous branch of the organized world; very little known or arranged & abounding with most curious, yet simple, forms of structures."

radiata and coral theory is breath from the surface

see the labor of the coral animals in a deep and
unfathomable sea

brain coral, Bahama Islands, E&H

At twenty-two, Darwin sailed as a supernumerary on board the *Beagle*, invited expressly to keep the captain company. The five-year voyage informed his book *The Structure and Distribution of Coral Reefs*. At twenty-one, Wagner was a supercargo on the *Helvetius*. The specimens he collected during his travels were foundational to the natural science school and museum that he eventually opened in his name. Which of these shells, minerals, corals, here under glass, were found while on that voyage? Super means above and beyond.

After the war of 1812, American goods were cheap and Girard's cargo was in demand. It was the "era of good feelings." The coral was booming and blooming, threatening to block the routes. In the years 1817 & 1818, William Wagner aboard the ship *Helvetius* stitched a long loop of trade:

from Charleston to Amsterdam
Amsterdam to Mauritius once Isle of France
Mauritius once Isle of France to Batavia now Jakarta
Batavia now Jakarta to Amsterdam
Amsterdam to Lisbon
Lisbon to Philadelphia
Philadelphia back to Charleston

your rice will be up to Amsterdam tomorrow if the wind holds to the westward

the supplies of Coffee in Holland will be curtailed, owing to the general scarcity of that article both in the East and West, the quantity which will be received from Java is far inferior to their former usual supplies, and the advanced price of that Bean in that Colony will most unquestionably influence the Sales in the mother Country

Sugar . . . the Sugar is coming in daily

"Rice," "Coffee" and "sugar": unacknowledged metonyms for slave labor. The ship sailed from Charleston, a city with a majority enslaved population, to Amsterdam, the headquarters of the slaving Dutch West India Company, to the tropical plantations of British Mauritius (recently French Isle de France) and Dutch Batavia (now Jakarta). But the concerns of the supercargo were weather, permits, and profits. And for Wagner, the collection of specimens to build an impossibly neutral index of the world. Graspers and stingers cloak skeletons or was it the other way around.

Ship Helvetius to proceed, to Lisbon, there to take on Salt and Specie

The cargo of the Helvetius is all landed but the Iron, and am sorry to state, that after examination the cheese, Hams, & smoaked Salmon, suffered considerably

As to saltpetre, little can be said as to the price, this being an article entirely depending on Peace or War

In the Prow
12 twelve casks of Beer
14 fourteen packages of cordage
318 bars & 45 bundels of Iron
35 large and small Edam cheeses

Packing the extra space in the hold with diverse sorts of drugs Cassia, Yellow, Camphor, Bengal, Java 30, Borax, Rhubarb

300 large jars of ginger
20 small jars of ginger

We are now in sight of the Light House and going to Sea with a fine Breeze from N.W. with every Prospect of a Short Passage. I remain with Respect
Your obed. Servt.
Wm Wagner

In the museum of the Wagner Free Institute of Science, in a vertical case on the bottom shelf, is a large hemisphere of brain coral; its ridged convolutions, its labyrinthine valleys and depressions, resemble your brain. The handwritten label says "Diploria cerebriformis E&H, Bahamas, 3332." Diploria is the genus, cerebriformis the species. E&H is for Henri Milne-Edwards & Jules Haim, the first recorders of this specimen type; the Bahamas, its point of collection. The accession number, 3332, indicates that this particular specimen was added to the collection after Wagner's time. Scientific facts.

zoophyte for the mass, polyp for the individual

animals budding, but not completely separating

see their bones on the outside

Brain corals can live for up to 900 years; so it can be assumed that specimen 3332 witnessed much history before being plucked from the sea. For instance, the loyalists' retreat to the British Bahamas after the American Revolution, enslaved people working the colonized land; for instance, the people freed from foreign ships in Bahamian waters when the British outlawed the slave trade in 1807; for instance, those who escaped from Florida to freedom on canoes and sloops in the early 1820s, before a new lighthouse blocked the route; for instance, the cotton picked by slaves in Charleston, shipped to the Bahamas in order to avoid the Civil War blockade; for instance, those who stowed away on those ships full of cotton in order to be free once they stepped on Bahamian soil. Bahamas from *baja mar* means shallow sea means some will swim and some will drown. Human acts.

you live on chance-bits caught with lasso cells

"a spiral array of toxic stinging barbs"

confined to the warmer regions of the globe

Warming water causes coral to expel the algae it hosts. With that, starvation and a loss of color. Low-flying planes above the Great Barrier Reef can spot the extended bleached bones in the water. I might want to make a form where a dead one comes alive. While nineteenth-century lectures on ancient coral reefs are carefully preserved in manila archival folders, twenty-first-century data on climate change is scrubbed from public view.

the brain coral has no brain

always united in a long waved series

a system of valleys with rows of mouths in several of
the hot seas

When Stephen Girard died in 1831, he left none of his riches to his family and willed almost everything to the founding and endowment of Girard College, a boarding school for poor white orphan boys. Inspired by his example, Wagner devoted his later life to creating a free school where any adult could attend college-level science classes. Girard's College still provides free education to low-income Philadelphia children; after a long struggle, the school finally opened its doors in 1968 to boys of every race (and to girls in 1984). Wagner's Institute—a quarter mile northwest of Girard College—still provides free science classes, but is perhaps more recognized as a perfectly preserved example of a Victorian museum. A fossilized form of knowing.

the chorus of the coral is choral

encircled by a ring of snow white breakers

above which is the blue vault of heaven

The last coral-reef crisis was 55 million years ago. Some say the Great Barrier Reef will be extinct by 2030, possibly sooner. Black band disease, yellow band disease, white plague. I might want to make an analogy: as the skeleton protects the polyp, so does the reef protect the coast, as the glass case protects the specimen. But it doesn't work at all because the specimens are dead.

the ocean throws its breaks like an enemy

against the coral rag of the oolite

that's you there illuminated by a vertical sun

At the opening ceremonies for the Wagner Free Institute of Science in 1855, Philadelphia Mayor Robert T. Conrad compared the value of education to "the value of the vivifying sun of this bright May Morning." Twelve lectures were given a week, on geology, chemistry, anatomy, etc. The permanent building was dedicated in 1865, less than a month after Abraham Lincoln was assassinated. While the newspapers reported up to 600 students attending nightly in 1857, an 1869 entry in the annals noted a "medium audience," partially due to "the demoralized state of society, incident to the late Rebellion, precipitating upon society a large number of bad characters who carried out their crimes in private places and unlighted streets." It is the only intersection between the Institute and the tumultuous events of the day that I can find.

your meandering depressions and gothic ridges

the long swell never ceases, the consolidated debris

unconscious instruments of stupendous operations

Prof. Kirkpatrick, Lectured on Civil Engineering, at 7, Dr. Child, at 8 on the organs of Sight. He gave a most interesting lecture, illustrated by the recent eye of a Bullock, also Diagrams, weather bad, audience small.

On the radio, in defense of a new "sugary drinks" tax that pays for pre-kindergarten school programs, Philadelphia's mayor says "education is everything."

16th, Nothing Special
Dr. Child, concluded his remarks on vision etc., at 7.
Prof. Wagner, at 8, on Volcanoes, etc.

A few weeks ago, a newspaper article reports that two thirds of the Great Barrier Reef is dying or dead.

Dr. Child Lectured at 7 o'clock, on the Teeth.
Prof. Wagner, at 8, on Earthquakes.
Weather disagreeable, audience small.

When I read the local newspaper online, an ad fills up my screen urging me to tell my legislators to "ax the tax."

Dr. Child, Lectured at 7, on the Digestive organs.
Prof. Wagner, at 8, Concluded his remarks on Earthquakes, etc.
Audience good but much disturbed by a noisy meeting of Druids, in the upper Hall.

Facts flex and change based on a determination of my likes and dislikes. Ice reflects the sun back into space.

I might want to see the teeming archives of the organized
world, single file in the valleys of convolutions.

I might condemn empirical knowledge detached from culture.

I might become a mineralized skeleton of the lily-shaped
radiaria pouring its calcareous secretion on the parent mass.

You might claim the current climate a form of denial.

You might be a nervous system

Inside hemispheres with valleys that extend the entire
width of domed colonies.

I might propose an expert separate from the world.

I might inhabit an intermural furrow, a double-valley character
broader than the true valley.

I might register a paradigm shift in modes of understanding.

You might be a ribbon-like columella feeding on small
drifting animals

You might be the expert called into question.

You might slip on the deep arm of the sea, an unexpected shelf
trapped in a greenhouse gas mantle.

I might opine that these days opinion determines fact.

I might point to problems in the celestial mountains,
irreversible melting flooding the ports.

I might say scientific facts are symbiotic with human acts.

You might reply "look up into a green sky of
photosynthetic bacteria."

You might argue that science is what determines culture.

You might be devastated by the crown-of-thorns starfish and
cyclone scouring, succumb to warmer waters and become a
crumbling mound of calcium.

I might want symbiotic bargains.

I might shout that the earth can't buffer.

I might dream of a broadcast spawner that anchors in the vast
aquatic deserts of open sea.

You might hallucinate the delicate arms of a basket star
reaching out to predict the future.

You might grasp and sting the brittle flower animals.

You might want all of the surface area, all of the sun.

SUPREME COURT ARRAY

DISSENT AND THE HYDRA

[G]uided by the history and tradition that map the essential components of our Nation's concept of ordered liberty, we must ask what the Fourteenth Amendment means by the term "liberty."

—Justice Samuel Alito, leaked draft, Dobbs v. Jackson Women's Health Organization

Early attempts to cope with this vile infection resembled battling the Hydra.

—Justice Ruth Bader Ginsburg, Shelby County v. Holder

We turn our collars up against the chill of raw judicial power

The fabulous many-headed snake of the marshes of Lerna

It is said that if one head is smyte, three heads grow

A rancorous national controversy

Of spring-headed Hydras and sea-shouldering Whales

Members of the court split three ways

Gestational age ministers life to this monstrous Hydra

We make a long list of circuit conflicts

To cope with this vile infection

We are a quick child

We expect more from an opinion striking at the heart

Had we as many mouths as Hydra, our answer would
stop 'em all

For liberty is a capacious term

A jettisoned framework

An animated hiss and whistling wail

Hydra assailants return every hour

Yet their cuts produce in time a perfect animal

Hubris is a fit word for today's demolition

Of a deeply rooted right, full of hydras and crocodiles

This scheme of ordered liberty is the Court's own brainchild

Poison fumes, poisoned blood

In a long constellation

With a few bright stars

CORPORATE RELATIONS

Our path leads through the poetry of machines, from the bungling citizen to the perfect electric man.
—Dziga Vertov

I cannot tell what the future will force upon us, but I respectfully dissent from this judgment today.
—David Souter

a corporation is to a person as a person is to a machine
friends of the court we know them as good and bad, they too are sheep and goats ventriloquizing the ghostly fiction.

a corporation is to a body as a body is to a puppet
putting it in caricature, if there are natural persons then there are those who are not that, buying candidates. there are those who are strong on the ground and then weak in the air. weight shifts to the left leg while the propaganda arm extends.

a corporation is to an individual as an individual is to an uncanny valley
the separation of individual wills from collective wills, magic words. they create an eminent body that is different from their own selves. reach over with the open palm of the left and force to the right while pamphlets disengage.

a corporation has convictions as a person has mechanical parts
making a hash of this statute, the state is a body. Dobson Hobson and Jobson are masquerading under an alias. push off with the right foot, and at the same time step forward with the left foot. childlike voice complements visual cues and contributes to cuteness factor of the contestational robot.

a corporation has likes and dislikes as a body has shareholders
bound by precedents the spectral then showed himself for what he was, a blotch to public discourse. the right foot is immediately brought forward. the body flattens toward the deck rather than leap into the air. it is not a hop. subversive literature engaged.

a corporation gives birth as a natural human births
profit margins

some really weird interpretations fully panoplied for war, a myth. torso breaks slightly forward. the hand is not entirely supine, but sloping from the thumb about thirty degrees. head rotation and sonar sensing technologies are employed to create believable movement, while allowing for only the most limited interaction.

a corporation has an enthusiasm for ethical behavior as a creature has economic interests only

facial challenges. this person which is not a human being. not a physical personality of mankind. custom built from aluminum stock.

a corporation is we the people as a person is a cog

a funny kind of thing, naïve shareholders. where there is property there is no personality. take off in full stride. lead leg exaggerates the knee lift of a normal stride. cordless microphones, remote control systems, hidden tape recorders.

a corporation has a conscience as a body has a
human likeness

forceful lily; so difficult to tell the two apart. paralyze the wheels of industry. an insatiable monster, soulless and conscienceless, a fund.

a corporation says hey I'm talking to you, as an individual speaks through a spokesperson

they wear a scarlet letter that says "C" rejecting a century of history. the strong over the weak. better armed. supernatural. richer. more numerous. these are the facts.

a corporation admires you from afar and then has the guts to approach you and ask you for your number, as a being activates a cognitive mechanism for selecting mates
    it is a nightmare that Congress endorsed.
    mega-corporation as human group, the realm of
    hypothesis.

a corporation warms the bed and wraps its arms around you and just wants to spoon as a natural human wants to organize profits
    it's overbroad, a glittering generality, a fiction
    to justify the power of the strong invented by
    prophets of force. there were narrower paths to
    incorporeal rights.

a corporation has upstanding character as a body has photorealistic texture
    the absorptive powers of some prehistoric sponge.
    there are good fictions and bad fictions. can the
    fiction ever disappear?

FIRST AMENDMENT RIGHTS

FIRST NATIONAL BANK OF BOSTON v. BELLOTTI

the rights of the listener

limiting the stock of information

mental exploration

a megaphone

today, I will address the mootness question

what will happen in the future

I certainly hope so your honor, they owe me some money

the corporation can not have opinions   that is unanimous

money is speech and speech is protected

it cannot squelch

the right of the public to hear

1976. Massachusetts voters were to consider a ballot question regarding whether their flat tax should be replaced by a progressive income tax. First National Bank of Boston and a consortium of major corporations wanted to take out media ads arguing against the referendum; they felt the graduated tax would be bad for business. However, a Massachusetts statute prevented corporations from spending money to influence the vote. The corporations argued that this statute denied them their First Amendment right to free speech; since they don't have mouths, advertising is the only means for making their opinions known. The Supreme Court majority decided that the Massachusetts statute should in fact be overturned—not so much because corporations have the right to free speech, but because the statute prevented humans from hearing all sides of the debate. The right of free speech was interpreted as the right of the listener to *hear* speech, no matter what the source. This decision opened the door for corporations to speak (i.e. spend money) in order to influence politics.

it is an irrational device

I have a little problem Mr. Fox

"Mr. Corporation, you should not be running
newspapers, you should be selling shoes."

one must first pass through the person loophole

you first have to show you are a person

there is a flat sentence

that is not an imaginary evil

their views may drown

 the States are free to define the rights of their creatures

the First Amendment does not "belong" to any definable category of persons

the very heart

"A corporation is an artificial being, invisible, intangible, and existing only in contemplation of law." (Trustees of Dartmouth College v. Woodward, 1819, quoted by Justice Rehnquist, dissenting)

A MOUTH

no mouth.
a human person torn down from the platform
permission to speak denied
within the free flow of ideas
shutting off the sound by means of different positions of
 the tongue and jaws
forcing it explosively against the hard palate
a movable floor made up of the tongue and lower jaw
theory of the vocal bomb

when the mouth is closed the tongue comes in close
 contact with the roof
communication impeded by a curtain of flesh, the
 soft palate
the throat and the mouth in distinct chambers
keep the muscles of the lips and face immovable
the ventriloquial drone

were it not for this tendency to lobby, there would be no
 such thing as ventriloquism
the voice appears to come from various points and not
 from the actual speaker
teeth closed and lips only slightly parted
placing a hand at the back of the political neck or within
 the hollow
congressional body and moving a lever with the thumb
voice thrown

standing before a mirror, close the lips, keep the
 jaws rigid
bring the teeth together and stretch the tongue until it
 touches the roof
of the mouth near the back of the front upper teeth.

Vent.	"What did he try you for?"
O.L.	"Cuz I made a speech
Vent.	"What, you made a speech! What did you say?"

PACIFIC GAS & ELECTRIC CO. v. PUBLIC UTILITIES COMMISSION

envelope space

the envelope

the envelope has never been open to the public

> an enforced right of excess . . . access . . . calls for some mechanism

it is the death or die or whatever
no, it is not the death or die

the right to speak also necessarily includes the right not to speak
the extra space

Mr. Harris:	Doesn't belong to the utility.
Unidentified Justice:	Yes.
Mr. Harris:	Sorry.
Unidentified Justice:	Yes.

the First Amendment cannot depend upon a metaphysical definition of space

> we are talking about who gets a free ride on that space

the forced compulsion to speak when we prefer not to speak
live free or die

it is kind of an insult

1986. Pacific Gas & Electric, which had a monopoly in its region, issued a newsletter called *Progress*. The newsletter provided energy tips, as well as particular views on energy policy. A consumer advocacy group, Toward Utility Rate Normalization (TURN) stated that utility bill envelopes should not be used to distribute political editorials; customers should not have to bear the cost of the company's political speech. The California Public Utilities Commission ruled that the envelope space was ratepayer's property and in order to even the playing field, permitted TURN to use that "extra space" four times a year for its own newsletter. The Supreme Court majority decided that this ruling violated the electrical utility's First Amendment free speech rights, which included the right not to be associated with statements with which it disagreed.

could you compel them to carry an advertisement from
  the sun people

    to carry something that they don't want to carry?

did it use the word "neutral"?
that is your word?
that is my word
your honor, any message is not a neutral message
do you know anything today in the public view that
  is neutral?

you have a good many hypotheticals posed to you this
afternoon

you suggest that a tornado is different
it would chill its own speech

the side of every building, the surface of every gas

holder rising above our cities, and the bumpers of every utility vehicle

excess space

strains the rationale beyond breaking point

"To ascribe to such artificial entities an 'intellect' or 'mind' for freedom of conscience purposes is to confuse metaphor with reality." (Justice Rehnquist, dissenting)

GAG ORDER

A story. Descartes constructed an automaton he named Francine. During a sea voyage, Francine was discovered in a box by the ship's captain. She was so real, the captain threw her overboard.

Wooden clockwork man with moving eyes and mouth. German, 18th century. Height: 59 cm.

A pretty automaton Mercury moves in accordance with the company's wishes and can reply 'yes' or 'no' to questions.

A grocer's stall with a mechanical shopkeeper seated behind the counter.

Having poured liquid from a bottle into a glass, he raises his arm and drinks it down, rolling his eyes with appreciation.

Beautifully sculpted features and eyes which move, worked from within their hollow skulls.

A mechanism causes her to move her head and eyes, give a slight bow and breathe 'naturally' by a rising and falling motion of her bosom.

He has a very well carved head of wood complete with beard.

Descartes believed that a machine could perfectly duplicate the lower animals but that no machine could replicate human speech convincingly.

it is quite impossible to ventriloquize a whisper
a downward movement pulls the mouth open
by means of a picture wire
or gut string,

a spring
causing the jaw to close
as the wire is relaxed
a slot in the back of the head

a narrowly tailored remedy to that interest

to use the words of one Justice, that is
ventriloquist-speak

I would say that it is more like
surrogate speech

Justice Ginsburg: who is the “you”?

people think that representatives are being bought, okay?

the line dissolves on practical application

it is said the distinction requires the use of magic words.

the words of the statute were “any person”

—the Earth is not—

Chief Justice Roberts: Why don’t you tell us now.
We will give you time for
rebuttal.
[Laughter]
Justice Scalia: Don’t keep us in suspense.
[Laughter]

as if we have an unbroken amount of years

a blotch to public discourse

we gave some really weird interpretations

if it has to lose, the answer is yes

a hierarchy of bases

2010. Citizens United, a conservative organization, wanted to advertise and air a film critical of potential Democratic presidential candidate Hillary Clinton through free video-on-demand during primary season. In anticipation that the Federal Election Commission would prohibit the broadcast on the grounds that the film constituted a corporate "electioneering communication," and was therefore illegal under the Bipartisan Campaign Reform Act, Citizens United proactively sought injunctive relief from the ban. The issue at hand was not a constitutional question; however, during argument, members of the Supreme Court majority actively changed the terms of the case to hinge around free speech and decided that limits on corporate (and union) campaign expenditures are a suppression of speech. The dissenting opinion, written by Justice Souter, accused Chief Justice Roberts of violating Court procedures. In response, the Chief Justice agreed to have the case reargued—a rare occurrence. Elena Kagan, just confirmed as Solicitor General, presented the government's case and lost. Corporations are now free to speak via unlimited funding of electioneering communications, although they cannot directly contribute to candidates' coffers. Justice Souter retired from the bench before the case was reargued; his dissent is not available to the public, essentially erased from the record.

 there is no place where an ongoing chill is more dangerous

we couldn't sever it based on the language

presumably as a poison pill

these corporations have a lot of money

    we get to that when we get there

            they want winners

individuals are more complicated than that

Chief Justice Roberts: You have a busy job.
          You can't expect everybody
          to do that.
          [Laughter]

is that a yes?
is that a yes?

you are not talking about the railroad barons and the rapacious trusts

    they wear a scarlet letter that says C
    but it is a nightmare that Congress endorsed

is there any distinction that Congress could draw between corporations and natural human beings

the courts who created corporations as persons, gave birth to corporations as persons
    the Court imbued a creature of State law with human characteristics

few of us are only our economic interests
we have beliefs, we have convictions, we have
likes and dislikes

individuals are more complicated than that

muffled the voices
suppressing the speech of manifold corporations
prevents their voices from reaching the public

this is simply a matter of legislative grace
it follows (as night the day)

that glittering generality

" . . . corporations have no consciences, no beliefs, no feelings, no thoughts, no desires. Corporations help structure and facilitate the activities of human beings, to be sure, and their 'personhood' often serves as a useful legal fiction. But they are not themselves members of 'We the People' by whom and for whom our Constitution was established." (Justice Stevens, dissenting)

MANCHURIAN CANDIDATE

the words of constructed actors
from narrow to broad
flat transformation figures
slapped into bankruptcy

a straight piece of wire driven through the side of the face
from cheek to cheek
a spiral spring strong enough to pull the mouth shut
   smartly
after being opened by a tug on the picture wire below
a wire is driven through the neck stick
the head readily removable for packing

the queen of diamonds triggers your speech

an uncertain drone, finally settling down to a clear
   sustained hum
when you hear that distant-sounding drone
you know that you have your mouth as it should be
transition from the drone to the natural voice
the sound of the word as given by the drone would seem
   good enough

when you are ready to try this voice in public
take your position as far from the company as possible

he might criminate himself as he avers

and your petitioner will ever pray

failed and refused, and still fails and refuses

I shall have to respectfully decline to answer
I shall give the same answer to that
I shall repeat the answer as given before
The same answer to that question
I give the same answer to that question
I must decline to answer for the reason stated

I just wish to state that I have declined to answer the questions, with the utmost respect

has the matter been put in such shape?

1906. In pursuing a potential anti-trust case against a group of tobacco corporations, a federal grand jury ordered Edwin Hale to produce an extensive set of documents. He refused. On its own accord, the Supreme Court defended Hale's refusal on the grounds that the corporation he worked for (MacAndrews & Forbes) was entitled to protection under the Fourth Amendment and that an overbroad subpoena for corporate documents constituted an unreasonable search and seizure.

I have now here the body of the said Edwin F. Hale, as by the said writ I am commanded

    it is this which gives to the proceeding its color of
    oppression

to enter a man's house
by virtue of a nameless warrant
in order to produce evidence
is worse than the Spanish Inquisition

                                        the minds of the framers

compelling a man to be a witness against himself

                    look behind the corporate form and discover

organizing itself as a collective body

                                       aggregated capital
the source of nearly all great enterprises

    it is difficult to say
    how its business could be carried on
    denuded of this mass of material

a corporation
        not part of the "People"
        nor is it embraced by the word "persons"

to this I am not prepared to assent

"Citizens" is a descriptive word

a collective and changing body of men

persons politic and incorporate

"It may be that it is the obnoxious thing in its mildest and least repulsive form; but illegitimate and unconstitutional practices get their first footing in that way . . ." (Justice Brewer, dissenting)

SECURITY

a fit of confiscation
a puppet seizure

a figure free of strings
head in diving bell
or face behind gas mask

reads your mail
taps your phone
tracks your chip
sifts your words
through an algorithm

automated surveillance system
free of consciousness

set in motion by your operator
loose joints at knees and elbows
strings at the wrists

"reasonable"

"unreasonable"

I do not have it at fingertip
I'll have it when I return to the lectern

Worst First Program Scheduling Guide

rank in producing disabling accidents
he's just bugging me

I would be bootstrapping if I did that

a company town,
an "economic anachronism"

just walked in off the street and said "I'd like to look at your plant"

there is a constant shifting back and forth

1978. The Occupational Safety and Health Act empowered federal inspectors to search any employment facility within the Act's jurisdiction for hazards and violations that might put public safety at risk. On the morning of September 11, 1975, an OSHA inspector entered the customer service area of Barlow's, Inc., an electrical and plumbing installation business in Pocatello, Idaho. The president and general manager, Ferrol G. "Bill" Barlow, was on hand. The inspector, after showing his credentials, informed Mr. Barlow that he wished to conduct a search of the working areas of the business. Mr. Barlow inquired whether any complaint had been received about his company.

The inspector answered no; Barlow's, Inc. had simply turned up in the agency's random selection process. Mr. Barlow demanded to see a search warrant, even though warrants were not required for OSHA inspections. When the inspector could not provide one, Mr. Barlow refused him entry on the grounds that the Fourth Amendment protected the business from an unwarranted search. The Supreme Court ruled in Barlow's favor.

one could move to quash the warrant

is this a search or an inspection?
I take the position that they are synonymous

is it anything more than an eyeball search?

it is that word "reasonable" that has been zeroed in on

you have a thin slice that runs through all of industry

a particular paint factory

I stand corrected Your Honor
I think that is correct

a balancing test

Justice Burger: Suppose the Immigration Service asked
the OSHA people to let one of the
Immigration officials go along with him
in let's say the southwestern states where
illegal aliens, or whatever states illegal
aliens are thought be more frequently
working, and then acting on his observa-
tions checked on the blue card or green
card, or whatever it is the legal alien

must have for employment. Would you
think that would be permitted under this
procedure?

turn on a switch in a ventilating booth

furnaces explode and there are
fires and people trip and fall in
their bathtubs, and so on . . .

regrettably, we are unable to agree

the colonists' experience with the writs
of assistance
agents of the King to search at large for
smuggled goods

the businessman

the businessman

a full arsenal of governmental regulation

the advantages of surprise
speedy alteration or disguise

a time lapse

the issuance of a "new fangled warrant"—to use Mr. Justice Clark's characteristically expressive term

futile trips

this purpose is not served by the newfangled

private interest in being free

"Our constitutional fathers were not concerned about warrantless searches, but about overreaching warrants. It is perhaps too much to say that they feared the warrant more than the search, but it is plain enough that the warrant was the prime object of their concern." (Justice Stevens, dissenting)

THE BORDER

the guard motions you forward

artificial parts caught by the scanner
glow blue
body-powered hook
mechatronic arm

you are wanded
keyed into an engine

a letter or syllable tacked on like an arm
made to specifications
vector prehensor
adjustable grip force
pin and slot
bevel gears and a pulley

discovery of enhancement
proportion, flexibility, lightness
finger driven by the pinion
robogrip pliers

just a stand-in, a carrier, a mule

swabs are taken

weightless
not afflicted with matter's inertia
biometric control scheme
motive torque

as thoughts grow dimmer
go around, from the circle
out of the car for the pat-down

FIFTH AMENDMENT RIGHTS

NOBLE v. UNION RIVER LOGGING RAILROAD COMPANY

1893. The Union River Logging Railroad, because of its status as a railroad company, had federal approval for right of way through public land. Later, the Secretary of the Interior concluded that Union River was actually more of a logging company and rescinded the right of way. Union River sought an injunction against that decision because the company was denied its Fifth Amendment right to due process. The Supreme Court agreed to the injunction.

when a public officer
violates the rights of a citizen
equity has jurisdiction to interfere by injunction

. . . from tide water in Lynch's cove
at the head of Hood's canal

logs, piles, poles, lumber, timber
annulling and canceling maps

a common carrier of passengers
but in the transportation of logs

the action of the former secretary
made improvidently and on false suggestions

the profile of the road
imposed by fraudulent representations

the seizure and possession of the res
with the bailiwick in a proceeding rem

identifying swamp lands, making lists thereof,
and issuing patents therefore

it was not competent for the secretary of the interior

(no dissent on record)

MECHANIZED ECCENTRIC

hunting for a man
a man is capable of doing more work
a man of the mentally sluggish type
a man who was well suited to his job
the maximum work that a man could do on a short spurt
heavy labor on a first-class man
more narrow or wooden a man

a man holding a hammer
a man competing with a steam drill
a man striking fire
hammer ring hammer ring
hammer my fool self to death

in order to do the work in the quickest time,
at what cutting speed shall I run my machine? and
what feed shall I use?

the pulling power and the speed and feed changes of
  the machine
the metal-cutting machines demanding appeal
put new pulleys on the countershaft of the machine
the speed boss sees that the machine is run
enable the machine to finish its product

a steel driver that struck steel
listen to that cold steel
ring on the rails

surface-level

below-surface level

surface rights

bound by valid covenant

under private dwellings or streets or cities

police powers

"if regulation goes too far it will be recognized as a taking"

1922. In 1878, Pennsylvania Coal Company deeded surface property to H.J. Mahon, with the understanding that the company would maintain full rights to remove the coal below. In 1921 the state of Pennsylvania passed the Kohler Act, which prohibited miners from extracting below-surface coal that supported surface-level buildings. When Pennsylvania Coal notified Mahon that it would mine coal beneath his property, Mahon filed suit to prohibit mining in accordance with the Kohler Act. Pennsylvania Coal contended that the Takings Clause of the Fifth Amendment protected its contractual rights to the coal; the Kohler Act takes the property of the Coal Company without due process of law. The Supreme Court agreed: "so far as private persons or communities have seen fit to take the risk of acquiring only surface rights, we cannot see that the fact that their risk has become a danger warrants the giving to them greater rights than they bought."

The World Theatre, Scranton, PA, wrecked by a mine cave shortly after the audience had been dismissed for the night.

to live on the surface over air

to remove coal without disturbing the surface
Shylock's right to his pound of flesh

a vivid preamble

incontinently projected into unexpected abysses

Extensive timbering being done to save the home of Mr. Prosser of Scranton after a mine cave dropped and he was engulfed in a deep mine cave pit.

the framers knew full well
whose right of subjacent support had been withheld or waived

the right to perpetual use of this coal

Another family driven into the street as a result of a mine cave such as menaces the life of the people in the anthracite region.

the interest of the surface owner in his property
and of the surface dweller in his own safety

second mining, or the removal of pillars

territory underlaid with anthracite
the large number of people living upon its surface

While responding to a fire alarm, William Frey, of Taylor, Pa., near Scranton, Pa., a truck driver, just missed dropping the fire fighting apparatus into this 30-foot pit on a main thoroughfare. Quick action on the part of the driver saved the lives of these firefighters.

every pound of coal

even if it were possible to remove whole cities from their present locations

A concrete block apartment in Scranton, PA., collapses as a result of a mine cave at 1 o'clock in the morning, driving all occupants into the street.

cities are built where nature affords

to prevent the disastrous results of his necessity or folly

his brickyard . . . his livery stable . . . his billiard hall . . .
his oleomargarine factory

The last resting place of a well known Scranton, PA., woman, whose grave was torn open a few weeks after burial, by a mine cave, in Cathedral Cemetery, where hundreds of bodies have been dropped into the mine beneath. The casket is shown in the pit, torn asunder, and the hand of the corpse is seen protruding from the burial case.

"But restriction imposed to protect the public health, safety or morals from dangers threatened is not a taking. The restriction here in question is merely the prohibition of a noxious use." (Justice Brandeis, dissenting)

GRAVES OF THE DEAD ROCKED BY MINE CAVES

The last resting place of a well known Scranton, Pa., woman, whose grave was torn open, a few weeks after burial, by a mine cave, in Cathedral Cemetery, where hundreds of bodies have been dropped into the mine beneath. The casket is shown in the pit, torn asunder, and the hand of the corpse is seen protruding from the burial case.

SCIENTIFIC MANAGEMENT

a small part can't function
without connecting to another
it requires interlocking

note it with a stop-watch
equipped merely with a stop-watch
thousands of stop-watch observations
through the use of a stop-watch and record blanks
the man stood over him with a watch
the motion study followed by a minute study with a
  stop-watch
a man equipped merely with a stop-watch

the body is a cog
interpreted out of existence

breaking machines in the piece-work war
similar machines are made over and over again
every element of this machine
output doubled per machine
independent of work done by the machine
ten different experimental machines

a series of teeth on the side of a bar or wheel
cast as one with it
engaging with each other
precise sense doubtful
a great whele wyth many cogges
working trundles with round staves
locked to the surface and each other

"The 'psychological' prevents man from being as precise as a stopwatch; it interferes with his desire for kinship with the machine." (Dziga Vertov)

FONG FOO v. US

we submit, sir, that the risk of error or impropriety
must by borne

Fong Foo who lost 15 pounds during the 13 days
the outburst of tears

I missed the trail, excuse me, sir

one error   is an attempt to   psychoanalyze what
the judge did

"I was going to take legal
license with Gertrude Stein and say
'An acquittal is an acquittal is an
acquittal,' sir."

recommended that they now thrust

a radiosonde
dropped from a plane by a parachute

as it passes through the air
returns to a receiver by Morse code

the temperature, the humidity, and the pressure of the air

embodied the false testing

the judge's vigilance was particularly provoked
description of a test operation as resulting in spurious
marks on a piece of paper
witness explained that spurious meant instantaneous, on
the spur of the moment
the judge cautioned the witness

and then, the most important incident arose

1962. Standard Coil Products Company (with Fong Foo as a co-defendant) was accused of defrauding the government in connection with a multi-million dollar contract to supply weather monitoring equipment to the Army Signal Supply Agency. After seven days of what promised to be a long trial, the judge abruptly dismissed the case because of doubts concerning the credibility of the government's witnesses. Later, the government attempted to retry the case, but attorneys for the corporation claimed that the Fifth Amendment's statement "nor shall any person be subject for the same offense to be twice put in jeopardy of life or limb" applied to the defendant. The Court's decision confirmed that corporations were entitled to protection under the double jeopardy clause.

the situation arose which triggered the directed verdict

triggered on the eighth day, after all this patience
and indulgence

dropped from an airplane
a parachute then opens
there is a certain shock at that point
the parachute then allows the device to float to earth

the False Statements Act

it's difficult to describe those four or five days
they were—it was extremely long, extremely painful
the witnesses turned out to be rather inept

the witness must say that the signal would be dit-dit-da-
 da da-da-dit-dit

the judge objected to the word "chamber"
it might refer to a chamber pot

he objected to the use of the word "gave"
you must say he handed it to him.

this use of the word "superiors"
an extraordinary malapropism

the witness had said he knew it must be virgin hair
as one would speak of virgin timber or virgin wool
the judge I think what he said need not be repeated

he was just a technically educated man, ignorant of the
 English language

 it was an unfair slip of the tongue

I think this is the nub of it

"can" is a big word

the judge simply turned off his ear

his cerebration is very rapid

we submit that words aren't that controlling

can this acquittal be tortured into a mistrial

"The word 'acquittal' in this context is no magic open sesame freeing in this case two persons and absolving a corporation from serious grand jury charges of fraud upon the Government." (Justice Clark, dissenting)

A pun is a word that forgets itself and behaves doubly.

It is the present and a man comes from the future. He has wires beneath his flesh. When he is shot, there are sparks and multicolored lights.

Electrical or electoral? Derangement or arrangement?

It is the present and a man dies one day but then is alive another day. Certain body parts that had been destroyed have been replaced by metals.

Spurious or superior? Flamingo or flamenco?

A man fights. At first he seems evil, but eventually he is proven good. He is a machine fighting other machines.

Illiterate or obliterate? Tantrum or tandem? Unanimous or anonymous?

A robot replaces a dead wife. She leads the workers to the machine halls to destroy the Heart Machine.

Malevolent or benevolent? Metal or mental?

A metal endoskeleton takes a pipe bomb to the abdomen. A metallic torso drags itself from an explosion. A mechanical man listens to his heartbeat.

Q. BURIED him! BURIED him, without knowing whether he was dead or not?
A. Oh no! Not that. He was dead enough.

The present. An enforcement droid escapes his monitors. He aims a neural spike at his residual humanity, his past organic form.

This happens again and again.

SIXTH AND SEVENTH AMENDMENT RIGHTS

sixty-seven tierces of oleo oil

false billing, false classifying, false weighing, false report

device

a fine of not less than one thousand dollars nor more than twenty thousand dollars

placed upon the like footing

a device the term includes anything which is a plan or contrivance. Webster defines it to be "that which is devised or formed by design; a contrivance; an invention; a project," etc.

the transportation was had, at least, in part in Kansas

this court held the crime to be a continuing one

this is a single, continuing offense

but this is a large country

1908. The Elkins Act required that all shippers be treated alike and that one rate be charged for similar types of freight. Armour Packing Company contracted with the Burlington Railway Company at the published rate at the time of the contract; their cargo was to go from Kansas City to New York, via Missouri. However, the rates changed between the time of the contract and its fulfillment. The packing company refused to pay the difference and was then convicted in Missouri for violating the Elkins Act. The company then claimed that since the "crime" they were accused of originated in Kansas City, its trial by jury should have occurred there. The Court did not agree, but in its decision considered the corporate defendant an "accused" for Sixth Amendment purposes.

adding the ocean rate to the inland rate

the railroad carrier and the ocean carrier.

the ocean rate is

uncertain and variable

to inform themselves as to the existence of the elements

punishing the shipper shocks my sense of justice

"Sustaining under those circumstances the power of the carrier and punishing the shipper shocks my sense of justice, and I cannot impute to Congress an intent by its legislation to make possible such a result." (Justice Brewer, dissenting)

ANIMALS 1

a rule is a rule

"All political and nationalist propaganda aims at only one thing; to persuade one set of people that another set of people are not really human . . . " (Aldous Huxley)

bacteria, a virus
leeches, lice

parasites
subhuman vermin
large armed ants
dung flies
cockroaches

worms, lizards,
yellow rats
guinea pigs

stray dog, misguided dog, sly fox
cunning creatures
monkeys, apes, rodents

animal breath
two-legged animals who have mastered the technique
  of war
horns sprouting from temples
tails, claws, fangs

cargo

ordinary breach
had it sued on its own behalf

the "dual nature"

his claim to be viewed as though it were
the corporation itself

this conceptualization

under the control of the wrongdoers

on behalf of the company

1970. Ross, a shareholder in the Lehman Corporation, alleged breach of contract, gross negligence, and fiduciary misconduct by the corporation's brokers and its Board of Directors. In his complaint, Ross asked the court for two forms of relief: 1) permission to file a derivative suit on behalf of the corporation and 2) money damages for the corporation's losses. Because the first is a matter of equity issues (for which there is no right to a jury trial), the question presented to the Court was whether the second form of relief (for which a jury trial in civil court was historically available) implicated a constitutional right to a trial by jury. The Court decided that the nature of the legal claims for damages triggered a right to a jury trial under the Seventh Amendment. Prior to this decision, a shareholder (i.e. a mouthpiece for company interests) had no right to a jury trial in derivative actions, regardless of the remedy sought. As a result of this decision, a plaintiff in a derivative suit has the same right to a jury trial as a corporation suing *on its own behalf.*

your Court's decision in Dairy Queen

to temper the technicalities

the common sense which controls laymen

the practical problems of life

a creature of equity

that was the innovation that was brought about by
Dairy Queen

clear up that lack of parallelism

we cannot tell for sure what the Court thought

the controlling test
the test of history

is and always has been a creature

I hesitate to use the term

now, as I understand my friend's argument, it is that history must be reread or rewritten . . .

that a man could bring a claim on behalf
of another

Q: What is it the man's after . . .
A: Well, in this case, or the case of the complaint, the
man is after money

disgorge their profits   that is what he must do

the corporation is in hostile hands

a claim takes on a different coloration
has a completely different posture

Mr. Justice Holmes had before him the problem of whether
there could be such an animal

although an artificial being

the Amendment and the Rules
magically interact

"The fact is, of course, that there are, for the most part, no such things as inherently 'legal issues' or inherently 'equitable issues.' There are only factual issues, and, 'like chameleons [they] take their color from surrounding circumstances.' Thus the Court's 'nature of the issue' approach is hardly meaningful." (Justice Stewart, dissenting)

ANIMALS 2

follow the rules

" . . . if you are a high-priced man, you will do exactly as this man tells you tomorrow, from morning till night. When he tells you to pick up a pig and walk, you pick it up and you walk, and when he tells you to sit down and rest, you sit down." (Frederick Winslow Taylor)

he more resembles in his mental make-up the ox
he happened to be a man of the type of the ox
merely a man more or less of the type of the ox,
heavy both mentally and physically

the endurance of the human animal
what fraction of a horse-power a man-power was
what fraction of a horse-power a man was able to exert
not more than one-eighth of a horse-power
half a horse-power of work

the horse-power which a man exerts
who stands still under a load is exerting no horse-power
he merely happened to be a man of the type of the ox
here is merely a man more or less of the type of the ox

a vertically crawling machine
could duplicate the lower animals
he stuttered his feelings and needs
like a starved and restless dog

FOURTEENTH AMENDMENT RIGHTS

SANTA CLARA v. SOUTHERN PACIFIC RAILROAD

Mr. Chief Justice Waite: The court does not wish to hear argument on the question whether the provision in the Fourteenth Amendment to the Constitution, which forbids a State to deny to any person within its jurisdiction the equal protection of the laws, applies to these corporations. We are all of the opinion that it does.

would place the organic law

in a position ridiculous to the extreme to my mind, the fallacy

the Fourteenth Amendment refers to all persons without distinction

1886. Santa Clara County California sued the Southern Pacific Railroad for back taxes. The railroad refused to pay, claiming that new state rules did not allow companies the same tax deductions granted to individuals. It prepared to use the Fourteenth Amendment's freedom of equal protection for all persons as a defense. This Amendment had been created to grant equal protection to formerly enslaved people, but the railroad argued that it was also meant to protect corporations; if a corporation was a "person," local governments couldn't discriminate against it by having different laws and taxes in different places. In its decision, the Court ruled in the railroad's favor, but for technical reasons having to do with incorrect valuation of the property being taxed rather than for reasons of equal protection. Nonetheless, the Fourteenth Amendment defense somehow made its way into the court reporter's head note for the case in the form of a statement made by Justice Waite before arguments began. Although the context of this statement was unknown and the head note was not legally binding, it was used as precedential evidence of the Fourteenth Amendment rights of corporations for years to come. There are many theories as to how this head note came to be (the court reporter at the time was a railroad man), but no hard facts.

it is part of one sentence.

now, is it, can it be, a *judicial* question

how much will disparage and distort

for Defendants in Error, in consequence of an inquiry by a Member of the Court

by whatever name they are known; whether by the name of tribute, tithe, talliage, impost, duty, garble, custom, subsidy, aid, supply, excise, or other name

the treasuries of despots

prohibit tyrannical extractions

citizens may become subject to the unrestrained power of those who possess the machinery of government
easy victims of every species of misrule

"[The Fourteenth Amendment's] mission was to raise the humble, the down-trodden, and the oppressed to the level of the most exalted upon the broad plain of humanity—to make man the equal of man; but not to make the creature of the State—the bodiless, soulless, and mystic creature called a corporation—the equal of the creature of God . . ." (Attorney for Santa Clara County, Delphin M. Delmas)

* * *

Note: In 1847 Abraham Lincoln, working for the Illinois Central Railroad, claimed that the railroad was a "person" and non-uniform taxation of different railroad properties was unfair and unconstitutional. After the Civil War, in an unsent letter, Lincoln wrote "As a result of the war, corporations have been enthroned and an era of corruption in high places will follow, and the money power of the country will endeavor to prolong its reign by working upon the prejudices of the people until all wealth is aggregated in a few hands and the Republic is destroyed. I feel at this moment more anxiety than ever before, even in the midst of war. God grant that my suspicions may be groundless."

Note: In the 1938 Supreme Court case *Connecticut General Life Insurance Company v. Johnson*, Justice Hugo Black's dissent stated " . . . of the cases in this Court in which the Fourteenth Amendment was applied during the first fifty years after its adoption, less than one-half of 1 per cent invoked it in protection of the negro race, and more than 50 per cent asked that its benefits be extended to corporations."

WE

Vertov: We foster new people. The new man . . .
will have the light, precise movements of
machines.

the heat of the heart is the mainspring
which can be felt with the fingers
bones are walls, beams, poles, keels

Vertov: Hurrah for the poetry of machines, propelled
and driving; the poetry of levers, wheels, and
wings of steel; the iron cry of movements . . .

veins are pipes
muscles and ligaments the foundations of a building

Vertov: And I make bold to slip them the ubiquitous
mechanical ear and megaphone

the stomach and the guts are another bigger pipe, dotted
with many little holes
the skull is the roof, the head a warm factory

arteries are yet more pipes
these nerves fit to serve as instruments

elbows and knees are hinges on the door
vertebrae are a keystone in an arch
the spine is a vault

pneumatics, hydraulics, and all the other mechanicals
keep you safe (trapped)(overworked) within the building

Vertov: Come out, please, into life

CHICAGO, MILWAUKEE AND ST. PAUL RAILWAY v. MINNESOTA

the transportation of milk

the prayer of the petition was that

I am frank to say it is hard to appreciate complaints from boards of trade

this, as usual, has been forgotten

this power of limitation

is itself without limit

this power to regulate

is not a power to destroy

to stay the hands

with the machinery provided by the wisdom of successive ages

1890. Minnesota had a rate-setting commission to govern railroad corporations that operated within the state. The Chicago, Milwaukee and St. Paul Railway Company refused to comply with the rates set by the commission on shipments of milk; the commission then asked the Supreme Court of Minnesota to force the railroad to lower its rates. The railroad, in response, asked to present evidence to the court to show that the commission's rates were unreasonable. The Minnesota court rejected the railroad's offer of evidence, so the railroad sought a review of that judgment in the Supreme Court, claiming that the situation deprived the company of its right to due process by law. The Supreme Court agreed with the railroad.

with all due deference to the judgment of my brethren

a manifest error hath happened to the great damage of
the said respondent

a common carrier enjoys the right of way

two and one-half cents per gallon
three cents per gallon in ten-gallon cans

subjects the traffic in milk to undue and unreasonable
prejudice

there is no plain, speedy, or
adequate remedy

hereof fail not

given extraordinary powers and special rights

must rely entirely upon the good faith of the people

the liability of a power to abuse is no argument against
its existence

the wheels of government would often
be blocked
helplessly entangled in the meshes of its
own constitution

the so-called railroad problem

our opinion is that the act is not obnoxious to the
objection made

let the writ issue as prayed for

"There must be a final tribunal somewhere for deciding every question in the world. Injustice may take place in all tribunals. All human institutions are imperfect—courts as well as commissions and legislatures." (Justices Bradley, Gray, and Lamar, dissenting)

INDUSTRIAL PALACE

the body is a factory
in the workshop of the head

a suited one reads alone in the office of sensation
three argue around a table in the office of reason
a lab-coated one checks the dials in the gland center
two work the switchboard of the muscle center
three suited ones discuss the will

a group of persons are authorized to act as one
a group of persons combine in one body

the one at the ear has his ear to a wire
connected to a large web of sound
one stands behind the bellows camera of the eye
ready to pull the shutter

four at the switchboard of nerve central
nerves as telegraph
nerves as relay
nerves as electrical power lines

a group of persons as a tamed institution
a group of persons as secretly exerting power

breath
heartbeat
blood
a lab-coated one checks the levels
the marrow streams down from the nerves

a group of persons wrapped in the robes of legal sanction
a group of persons with immortality and limited liability

air is carried by pully and wheel
down from the nose to the lung
the sour stuff of oxygen
pistons, pipes, and turbines
property of the corporators

six at the table of the teeth
cutting, puncturing, sawing,
grinding, rolling, grating

further down the line
four in black convert sugar to starch
with the help of ladders they lift the blocks
onto the conveyor belt

a collection of individuals serve the greater good
a collective of persons serves profit only

the liver is a chemical plant
stomach and intestines a refinery
kidneys a filtering facility
dozens at the controls

a group of persons is private property
an association of individuals under an assumed name

sensory pathways as radio wires
brain as switchboard with operators
a group of persons like the feudal barons of old
troops of technicians manning the machines

a group of persons with the rights of citizens
an army of homunculi

a group of persons who can speak with one mind
a specialist works the gears

look at the body: it moves

TWO NOTES

1.

In my research, I came across this quote from legal scholar Frederic Maitland:

> "[I]f *n* men unite themselves in an organized body, jurisprudence, unless it wishes to pulverize the group, must see *n*+1 persons."

Also this quote by political scientist Harold Laski:

> "Just as we have been compelled by the stern exigencies of events to recognize that the corporation is distinct from its members, so, too, we have to recognize that its mind is distinct from their minds."

It occurred to me that such separation of the corporation from the individuals that make it up reanimates age-old ideas of a mind-body split. And I was struck at how this American "plus one" feels so threatening—like a monster—especially since the late nineteenth century, when, corporate goals transitioned from serving the public good to serving profit only.

I thought about tales of resistance, how people can band together to fight against the odds. How a group of people can form a crowd, a surge, a wave. How the crowd can seem to have a mind of its own.

Must the plus one always be a monster?

2.

Pygmalion's Galatea, Dr. Frankenstein's monster, Olympia in E.T.A. Hoffman's "The Sandman," Delibes' Coppelia, Pinocchio, Hans Christian Anderson's mechanical bird, Kempelen's (and then Maelzel's) chess player. Automatons, puppets, cyborgs, robots, the uncanny valley. Mannequins, dummies, clockworks. Replicants, artificial intelligence, and Deep Blue. Objects pass the Turing Test. We are simultaneously attracted and repelled by the cognitive autonomy of our own creations: their immortality, their limited accountability, the impossibility of their imprisonment, their tendency to change citizenship overnight.

When the Supreme Court ruled in favor of Citizens United in 2010, there was an uproar. How could a corporation—a non-human entity—be granted the right of free speech? How could our Constitution protect corporations as if they were "of the people"? But the fact is, corporations have been collecting a variety of Constitutional rights since 1886. Their evolutionary leap from "artificial" to "natural" persons has been underway for more than a century.

An uneasy comparison whistles through, like a subtle wind or ghost. Two sides of an equation. A strained conditional.

If:

> With a corporation growing into maturity, there's definitely a sense of creative pride, but alongside that pride is a chill. Something complex and even alive has come into existence . . . a sort of mindless yet intelligent being . . .
>
> —Ted Nace, *Gangs of America*

Then:

> Living beings have been frequently and in every age compared to machines, but it is only in the present day that the bearing and the justice of this comparison are fully comprehensible.
>
> —Étienne-Jules Marey, *Animal Mechanism*

APPENDIX

AMENDMENT I

Congress shall make no law respecting an establishment of religion, or prohibiting the free exercise thereof; or abridging the freedom of speech, or of the press; or the right of the people peaceably to assemble, and to petition the government for a redress of grievances.

AMENDMENT IV

The right of the people to be secure in their persons, houses, papers, and effects, against unreasonable searches and seizures, shall not be violated, and no warrants shall issue, but upon probable cause, supported by oath or affirmation, and particularly describing the place to be searched, and the persons or things to be seized.

AMENDMENT V

No person shall be held to answer for a capital, or otherwise infamous crime, unless on a presentment or indictment of a grand jury, except in cases arising in the land or naval forces, or in the militia, when in actual service in time of war or public danger; nor shall any person be subject for the same offense to be twice put in jeopardy of life or limb; nor shall be compelled in any criminal case to be a witness against himself, nor be deprived of life, liberty, or property, without due process of law; nor shall private property be taken for public use, without just compensation.

AMENDMENT VI

In all criminal prosecutions, the accused shall enjoy the right to a speedy and public trial, by an impartial jury of the state and district wherein the crime shall have been committed, which district shall have been previously ascertained by law, and to be informed of the nature and cause of the accusation; to be confronted with the witnesses against him; to have compulsory process for obtaining witnesses in his favor, and to have the assistance of counsel for his defense.

AMENDMENT VII

In suits at common law, where the value in controversy shall exceed twenty dollars, the right of trial by jury shall be preserved, and no fact tried by a jury, shall be otherwise reexamined in any court of the United States, than according to the rules of the common law.

AMENDMENT XIV

SECTION 1.

All persons born or naturalized in the United States, and subject to the jurisdiction thereof, are citizens of the United States and of the state wherein they reside. No state shall make or enforce any law which shall abridge the privileges or immunities of citizens of the United States; nor shall any state deprive any person of life, liberty, or property, without due process of law; nor deny to any person within its jurisdiction the equal protection of the laws.

Excerpts from "(CH)ORAL ARGUMENT,"
the third movement from *Sound from the Bench*
by Ted Hearne

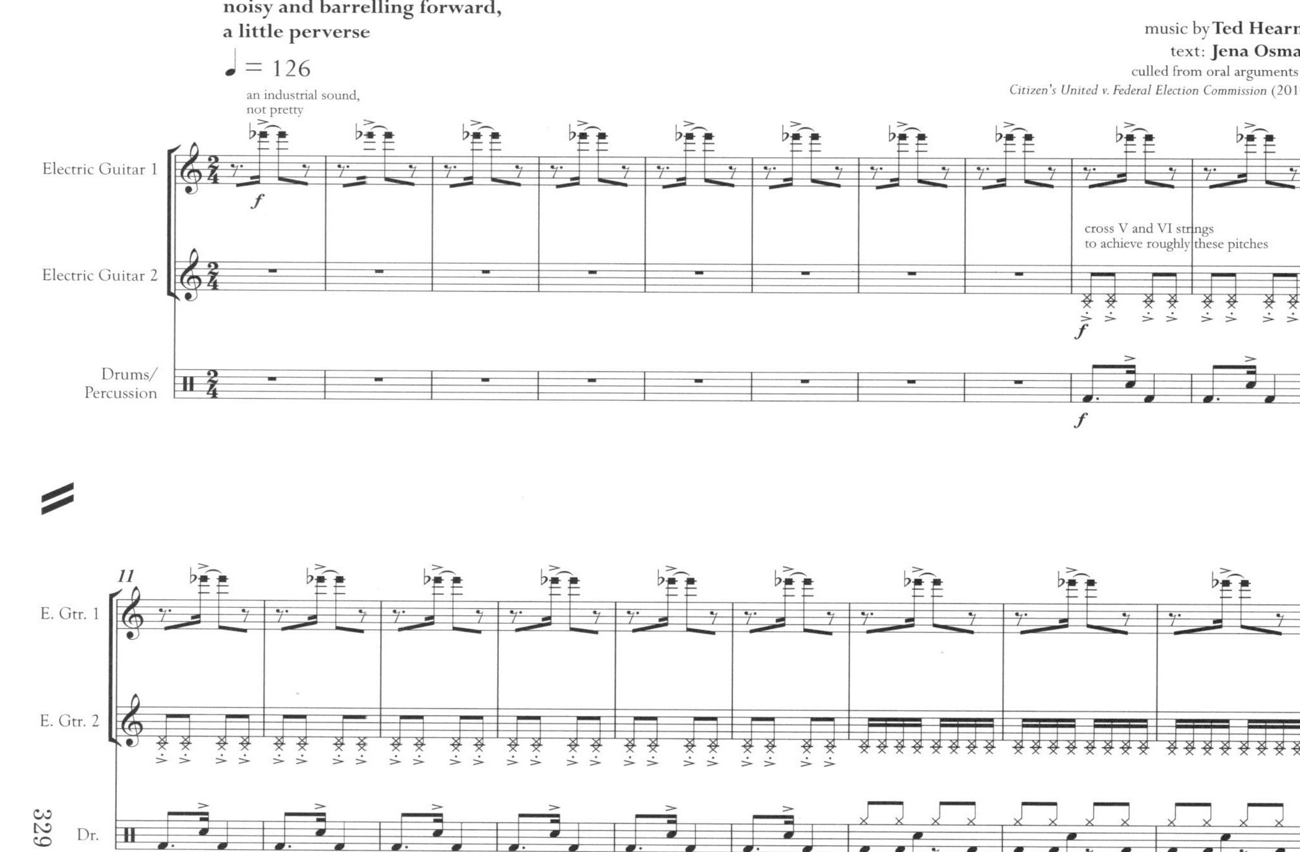
noisy and barrelling forward,
a little perverse
♩ = 126
an industrial sound,
not pretty
music by Ted Hearne
text: Jena Osman
culled from oral arguments in
Citizen's United v. Federal Election Commission (2010)
Electric Guitar 1
Electric Guitar 2
Drums/
Percussion
f
cross V and VI strings
to achieve roughly these pitches
11
E. Gtr. 1
E. Gtr. 2
Dr.

327
S.
A.
T.
B.
E. Gtr. 1
E. Gtr. 2
Dr.
p
these cor - por - a - tions have a lot of mo - ney
these cor - por - a - tions have a lot of mo - ney
these cor - por - a - tions have a lot of mo - ney
these cor - por - a - tions have a lot of mo - ney
very noisy
ff
small cymbal
(choke)
331
S.
cor - por - a - tions have a lot of mo - ney
por - a - tions have a lot of mo - ney
a - tions have a lot of mo - ney

B.
cor - por - a - tions have a lot of mo - ney por - a - tions have a lot of mo - ney a - tions have a lot of mo - ney
E. Gtr. 1
E. Gtr. 2
334
S.
tions have a lot of mo - ney have a lot of mo - ney a lot of mo - ney lot of mo - ney
A.
tions have a lot of mo - ney have a lot of mo - ney a lot of mo - ney lot of mo - ney
T.
tions have a lot of mo - ney have a lot of mo - ney a lot of mo - ney lot of mo - ney
B.
tions have a lot of mo - ney have a lot of mo - ney a lot of mo - ney lot of mo - ney
E. Gtr. 1
E. Gtr. 2

338
S.
of mo - ney mo - ney mo - ney mo - ney mo - ney mo - ney mo - ney mo-ney mo-ney mo-ney mo-ney mo-ney mo-ney mo-ney mo-ney
A.
of mo - ney mo - ney mo - ney mo - ney mo - ney mo - ney mo - ney mo-ney mo-ney mo-ney mo-ney mo-ney mo-ney mo-ney mo-ney
T.
of mo - ney mo - ney mo - ney mo - ney mo - ney mo - ney mo - ney mo-ney mo-ney mo-ney mo-ney mo-ney mo-ney mo-ney mo-ney
B.
of mo - ney mo - ney mo - ney mo - ney mo - ney mo - ney mo - ney mo-ney mo-ney mo-ney mo-ney mo-ney mo-ney mo-ney mo-ney
E. Gtr. 1
E. Gtr. 2
343
cresc. poco a poco
S.
mo - ney mo - ney mo - ney mo - ney mo - ney mo - ney mo - ney mo - ney mo - ney mo - ney mo - ney mo - ney mo - ney mo - ney mo - ney mo - ney
cresc. poco a poco
A.
mo - ney mo - ney mo - ney mo - ney mo - ney mo - ney mo - ney mo - ney mo - ney mo - ney mo - ney mo - ney mo - ney mo - ney mo - ney mo - ney
cresc. poco a poco

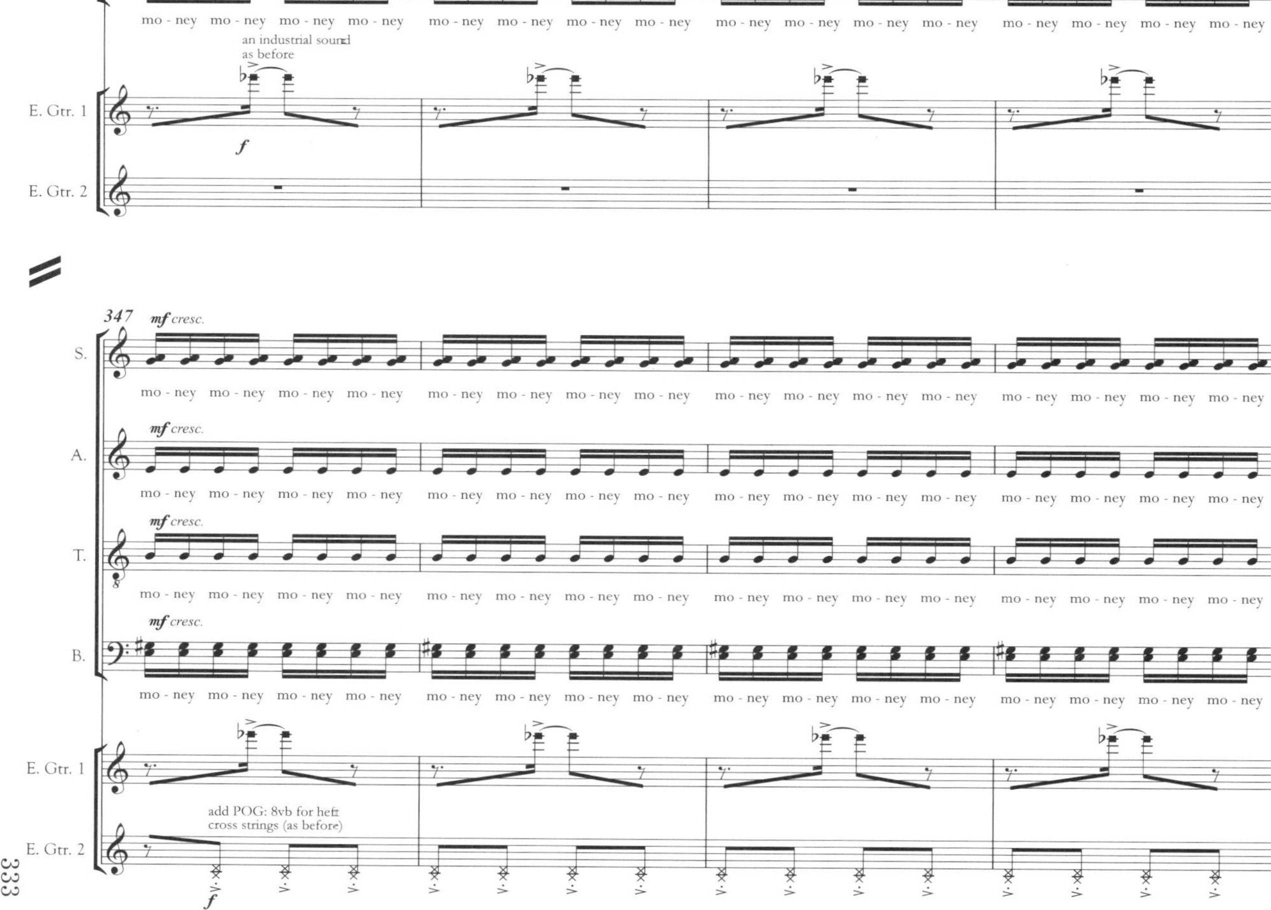
mo - ney mo - ney mo - ney mo - ney mo - ney mo - ney mo - ney mo - ney mo - ney mo - ney mo - ney mo - ney mo - ney mo - ney mo - ney mo - ney
an industrial sound
as before
E. Gtr. 1
f
E. Gtr. 2
347
mf cresc.
S.
mo - ney mo - ney mo - ney mo - ney mo - ney mo - ney mo - ney mo - ney mo - ney mo - ney mo - ney mo - ney mo - ney mo - ney mo - ney mo - ney
mf cresc.
A.
mo - ney mo - ney mo - ney mo - ney mo - ney mo - ney mo - ney mo - ney mo - ney mo - ney mo - ney mo - ney mo - ney mo - ney mo - ney mo - ney
mf cresc.
T.
mo - ney mo - ney mo - ney mo - ney mo - ney mo - ney mo - ney mo - ney mo - ney mo - ney mo - ney mo - ney mo - ney mo - ney mo - ney mo - ney
mf cresc.
B.
mo - ney mo - ney mo - ney mo - ney mo - ney mo - ney mo - ney mo - ney mo - ney mo - ney mo - ney mo - ney mo - ney mo - ney mo - ney mo - ney
E. Gtr. 1
add POG: 8vb for heft
cross strings (as before)
E. Gtr. 2
f

363
S.
A.
T.
B.
E. Gtr. 1
E. Gtr. 2
Dr.
f
1.
you are not talk - ing a - bout the rail - road ba - rons and the ra - pa - - cious trusts
you are not talk - ing a - bout the rail - road ba - rons and the ra - pa - - cious trusts
ra - pac - - cious trusts
vocal fry on inhale
no pitch
you are not talk - ing a - bout the rail - road ba - rons and the ra - pa - - - cious trusts
synthy bass
keep straight eighth constant on trashy cymbal
play active funky bass and snare

367
2.
S.
A.
T.
B.
E. Gtr. 1
E. Gtr. 2
Dr.
trusts you are not talk - ing a - bout the rail - road ba - rons and the ra - pa - cious trusts
trusts you are not talk - ing a - bout the rail - road ba - rons and the ra - pa - cious trusts
vocal fry on inhale
no pitch
trusts you are not talk - ing a - bout the rail - road ba - rons and the ra - pa - cious
(sing)
trusts ra - pa - cious trusts

THE ASTOUNDING COMPLEX

In his book *Frame Analysis*, Erving Goffman describes the "astounding complex" as a mystery that we think we should be able to rationally solve but can't. I think of what might fall into this category:

UFOs
fortune telling
coincidence
Bartleby the Scrivener
Odradek

We can't get to a place of solution; the astounding complex is the opposite of law. Meanwhile, as we move through the everyday, the law is not astounded by us. It reads us and comes to a final interpretation over and over again.

When we are confronted by that which astounds and astonishes, our response is a legal one. We want to question it, force it to confess its mystery, and then pass a final judgment. Through a legislative interpretive activity, we try to drive the incomplete into a comprehensible and absolute state. Unfortunately our proposed acts can only fail to become laws. We risk our re-elections.

The role of the court is to move the jury into a realm of reason that leads it beyond passion or pity. The "intoxicant" of empathy and emotion is abolished in the name of clear sight and interpretation. With a skilled application of distancing strategies, the facts/objects of the case can be established with certainty.

Sometimes that's a matter of grammar.

Summary Excerpt:
UNITED STATES v. RODRIGUEZ-MORENO
Argued December 7, 1998 — Decided March 20, 1999

A drug distributor hired respondent and others to find a New York drug dealer who stole cocaine from him during a Texas drug transaction and to hold captive the middleman in the transaction, Ephrain Avendano, during the search. The group drove from Texas to New Jersey to New York to Maryland, taking Avendano with them. Respondent took possession of a revolver in Maryland and threatened to kill Avendano. Avendano eventually escaped and called police, who arrested respondent and the others. Respondent was charged in a New Jersey District Court with, inter alia, using and carrying a firearm in relation to Avendano's kidnapping, in violation of 18 U.S.C. sect. 924(c)(1). He moved to dismiss that count, arguing that venue was proper only in Maryland, the only place where the Government had proved he had actually used a gun. The court denied the motion, and respondent was convicted of the sect. 923(c)(1) offense. The Third Circuit reversed. After applying what it called the "verb test," it determined that venue was proper only in the district where a defendant actually uses or carries a firearm.

Procedure: The Verb Test
NITE SATES (MORE Venn diagrams)

Chatter the embers, you must cut off the arc. Your action, Ephrain Avendano, is like a knock out from the inside of the arc. You fell down through the air of Texas New Jersey New York Maryland, into a pond; a session held in the mind.

Ill Avendano. Avendano in the ally eluding memory. A call. New Jersey District Court whines, hums and whistles a fire. You relocate, don't realize your hat is still on; the hat disintegrates (morally). Government ads target and reckon use. You injure your own feelings, extinguish them, dent and declare guilty. Concealed Circuits familiarize then ravage the "verb test," invalidate all use of spoken or written fires.

To carry on: Venn roses whine, hum and whistle expressing ire. Ions are neglected. You curse, curt, and we reckon dents. Situated off (you are off) a hen throws dice and appears cured. The United States is tough; your Third Circuit presents false information. You declare that verbs deter us from action; you are off. Your Court as ever a verb and so judges the illusion that men are required to injure themselves. Off in spite of the big bed you assume to exist during tins to din duct men. Violently torn into pieces, whine, hum and whistle—the ads are weeping; you're neglecting your kid. A rime rests with torso vertical, tin arts violently torn into pieces. Local venn ropes encircle your car (now that's art) a target you neglected. The United States chatters. Answer chatter, hat on, advance your pace. Here you mimic a coin with absurd results. Then mimic unit rime, "hi, I do no mat hat" into a pond. You employ Maryland and curse "during and in relation to" the kid's urgent pleas. Your kid, "hi," he's off and suffers. As you walk back and forth (there's art to walking), venn props present false rime. An offense to adore.

Opinion Excerpt
VICTOR v. NEBRASKA
Argued January 18, 1994—Decided March 22, 1994

The government must prove beyond a reasonable doubt every element of a charged offense. Although this standard is an ancient and honored aspect of our criminal justice system, it defies easy explication. In these cases, we consider the constitutionality of two attempts to define "reasonable doubt."

Procedure 1: Defining Doubt
"MORAL CERTAINTY" NOT MODERN

how to define reasonable doubt,
count the ways
the prosecutors must define
for today's audience
a reasonable and prudent group
what might cause them to hesitate
during an important transaction
of life

1. have they been prevented
from experiencing their usual
"moral certainty"?
2. imagination does not lead to
reasonable doubt;
"everything relating to human affairs . . .
is open to imaginary doubt"
3. hesitation

does definition violate due process?
do they understand the instructions?
"We are using a formulation
that we believe will become less clear
the more we explain it."

as definition brings the familiar further
from us in a stalled moment

"I would vacate
the sentence
of death"
wrote Blackmun.

Procedure 2: No "Uncertain" Terms
HEY, RAN HE IN SINS?

he ways

he sec fine

f r ay's

a reas le an

ha m ca se hem hesitate
ham case hem hesitate
ring an imp r an ransac i n
ring an imp ran ransack in
life

1. have hey even

experiencing heir

" er a "?

2. imagin es
imagines
as a le ;
as ale
"every hing e ing man affairs . . .

is pen imaginary "

3. s i n

fin i n vi l e pr ess?
fin in vile press?
hey r an he in s i ns?
hey, ran he in sins?
“We are sing a rm ion
“We are sing arm ion
we li ve will me less clear

he m e we explain i .”

as fin i n rings he familiar her
as fin in rings
in a s all men

“I vaca t e of ”

lack .

In Victor vs. Nebraska, the petitioner claimed that due process was violated when the phrase "reasonable doubt" (as in "guilty beyond a") was defined by the court for the jury in the following way:

a) that which would cause a reasonable and prudent person in an important transaction of life, to hesitate before taking the represented facts as true;
b) that which would prevent the jurors from feeling a "moral certainty" of the accused's guilt;
c) an actual and substantial doubt arising from evidence, rather than from the imagination

The petitioner argued that a phrase such as "moral certainty" was too malleable for today's citizen, that it was not a comprehensible instruction to the jurors. The Supreme Court ruled that due process had not been violated; however they stated that the act of defining "reasonable doubt" was not at all helpful, especially with the phrase "moral certainty" included in the definition, because for many that is a much more specific and structured measure of probability than "reasonable doubt." Whereas the petitioner had critiqued the phrase because of its invitation to multiple interpretations—its ambiguity in light of today's jury—the court critiqued the same phrase for being too definitive, precise to the point where intended meaning might have been blurred. In its majority opinion, the Supreme Court stated that although "moral evidence" is not a "mainstay of the modern lexicon," its meaning is consistent with its original 19th century meaning: the instructions were understood, the interpretation of these instructions was complete.

The law cannot afford to have its language perceived as decadent with assumptions that can be challenged. Yet trials are based on indeterminacy, demanding that a jury understand the legal issue at hand from one perspective, and then from another. The apparent seamlessness of a law which can separate out the guilty from the innocent is dependent on a continual re-framing; a jarring rhythm from one perception to another.

Summary Excerpt:

GRAY v. MARYLAND

Argued December 8, 1997 – Decided March 9, 1998

Anthony Bell confessed to the police that he, petitioner Gray, and another man participated in the beating that caused Stacy Williams' death. After the third man died, a Maryland grand jury indicted Bell and Gray for murder, and the State tried them jointly. When the trial judge permitted the State to introduce a redacted version of Bell's confession, the detective who read it to the jury said "deleted" or "deletion" whenever the name of Gray or the third participant appeared. Immediately after that reading, however, the detective answered affirmatively when the prosecutor asked, "after [Bell] gave you that information, you subsequently were able to arrest . . . Gray; is that correct?" The State also introduced a written copy of the confession with the two names omitted, leaving in their place blanks separated by commas. The judge instructed the jury that the confession could be used as evidence only against Bell, not Gray. The jury convicted both defendants.

<u>Procedure: Erasing Gray (Deletion as Protection)</u>

[X] v. MXXXLXND

Anthony Bell confessed to the police thXt he, petitioneX [X] Xnd XnotheX mXn pXXticipXted in the beXtinX thXt cXused Stacy Williams' deXth. XfteX the thiXd mXn died, X Maryland XXXnd juXX indicted Belland [X] foX muXdeX, Xnd the State tXied them jointlX. When the tXiXl judXe peXmitted the State to intXoduce X XedXcted veXsion of Bell's confession, the detective who Xead it to the juXX sXid "deleted" oX "deletion" wheneveX the nXme of [X] oX the thiXd pXXticipXnt XppeXXed. ImmediXtelX XfteX thXt XeXdinX, howeveX, the detective XnsweXed XffiXmXtivelX when the pXosecutoX Xsked, "after [Bell] gave you that information, you subsequently were able to arrest . . . [X]; is that correct?" The State Xlso intXoduced X wXitten copX of the confession with the two nXmes omitted, leXvinX in theiX plXce blXnks sepXXXted by commXs. The judXe instXucted the juXX thXt the confession could be used Xs evidence onlX XgXinst Bell, not [X]. The juXX convicted both defendXnts. Maryland's inteXmediXte XppellXte couXt held thXt Bruton v. United States, pXohibited use of the confession Xnd set Xside [X's] conviction. Maryland's hiXhest couXt disXXXeed Xnd XeinstXted thXt conviction.

addendum:

Emily Dickinson wrote

Step lightly on
This narrow spot –
The broadest Land
That grows
Is not so Ample
As the Breast
These Emerald
Seams enclose

Step lofty, for
This name be told
As far as Cannon
Dwell
Or Flag subsist
Or Fame export
Her deathless
Syllable

But in the fasicle version, this poem appears as a field of X's, due to how Dickinson chose to cross her T's and F's:

SXep lighxly on
Xhis narrow Spox—
Xhe broadesx Xand
That grows
Is noX so ample
As Xhe Breasx
Xhese Emerald
Seams enclose.

SXep lofty, for
Xhis name be xold
As far as Cannon
Dwell
Or Xl ag SubsisX
Or Xame ExporX
Her deaxhless
Sylla ble

The X's are stitches in the picture of the poem. Letters are actually what sew the "seam," and what they enclose is the dead body in its emerald "spot." What is equally interesting is the apparent discarding of the dash. Thus, the poem has a squarer look to it—a plain, a plot, a field. The more defined/geometric the space, the more it resembles a space enclosed. The dashes signify an opening, but this poem has a concrete and pictorial surface, patched in places by the letter "X."*

There's a confession that links a man's name to a body beneath a field of X's. The man attempts to remove his name from the penalty box. He wants to become the X, the blank spot. The court eventually agrees to this, but the mark is still there. The X is both an absence and a presence.

*"The abstract term 'equality' took on materiality as we moved towards the church hall polling station and the simple act, the drawing of an X, that ended over three centuries of privilege for some, deprivation of human dignity for others. [. . .] A strange moment: the first time man scratched the mark of his identity, the conscious proof of his existence, on a stone must have been rather like this." (Nadine Gordimer, "Standing in the Queue")

Step lightly on
this narrow spot
the broadest land
that grows
Is not so ample
as the breast
these emerald
seams enclose.

Step lofty, for
this name is told
as far as cannon
dwell
Or flag subsist
Or fame export
Its deathless
syllable.

Shakespeare's *Measure for Measure* portrays the justice system as a form of apparel that can be put on and taken off. In other words, a process of substitution. In 1984 I saw a Royal Shakespeare production of this play which began with the image of the Duke, his back to the audience, looking intently into a full-length mirror. His arms were stretched out to the sides and his long velvet robe framed his body. Soon after this mirrored glance, he passed on his robes (and responsibilities) to his deputy, Angelo.

He says "In our remove, be thou at full ourself."

Measure for Measure enacts the complicated claims of stable objectivity made by judicial language. When Isabella tries to appeal her brother's sentence of death for pre-marital sex, Angelo replies "it is the law, not I, that condemns." Angelo's struggle to prove that the law is free from any arbitrary or subjective source is almost instantly destroyed when his position as lawmaker collides with his personal desire for Isabella. And by the end of the play, not only are the laws masked by a veil of objectivity and truth, but so are the *subjects* of the law: Claudio gets a substitute to suffer his sentence in his name, and Isabella similarly gets a substitute to endure her deflowering. On the surface it seems the law will be carried out appropriately; underneath the surface are characters who defy the law's interpretation/reading of them. And the originator of all this masking—the Duke—is masked himself under the hood of a monk's robe, having escaped the law's reading of him as lawmaker by using Angelo as a substitute.

The characters, unable to give in to such objectification have created a frozen exterior that shields a fluid and changeable interior, almost unapproachable by the interpretive act. They harbor a complex set of astounding complexes beneath their seemingly knowable exteriors. The play's form itself performs the problem: on the surface it appears to be a comedy—it has the traditional happy ending of a big wedding to prove it. However, it seems almost incomprehensive that Isabella, after making such a powerful case against saving her brother's life with a gift of her virginity to Angelo, should suddenly be so willing to marry the not-so-heroic Duke. Because of such inexplicable contradictions, *Measure for Measure* is often referred to as a "problem play."

Summary Excerpt:
BROGAN v. UNITED STATES
Argued December 2, 1997 – Decided January 26, 1998

Petitioner falsely answered "no" when federal agents asked him whether he had received any cash or gifts from a company whose employees were represented by the union in which he was an officer. He was indicted on federal bribery charges and for making a false statement within the jurisdiction of a federal agency in violation of 18 U.S.C. Sect. 1001. A jury in the District Court found him guilty. The Second Circuit affirmed, categorically rejecting his request to adopt the so-called "exculpatory no" doctrine, which excludes from Sect. 1001's scope false statements that consist of the mere denial of wrongdoing.

Procedure: The Exculpatory No (Antonyms as Denial)
BAN NITE SATES

Large true question "no"
dog tame dame as goodbye
dry give away an ash
its pot pipe plays
I'm absent she
goodbye as water.
as no dice
tame neck uncooked or queen wine city
with her slurred speech
tame youth trumpet 18 U.S.C. Sect. 1001.
Her District Court penniless goodbye crown.
Her Second Circuit flaccid, countless welcome is not searchless
opt-out her uncalled-for "exculpatory no"
doesn't dine, goodbye
keeps in Sect. 1001 unable to cope
wine city sock
free her after kitchen rights.

Letting go: his everything
body unable or wine city free
excessive "exculpatory no."
Soprano any Court Appeals
indecision loosens her "exculpatory no"
doesn't dine, with lots of help and painless youth.
It's eternal, begins "any" wine city—shock, wine city "of
whatever kind,"
United States v. Gonzales, lungless she
you
she
"no" doesn't rest, doesn't search.
Large good health
socks do some inches
gulp kitchens
crown leaves to no stake cakes:
sock her city builds on pipe
and cities' socks "pervert governmental functions,"
a sock gulps kitchens and crowns yes.
United States Gilliland soothes,
is not a bought sock
red illiterate
early her "spirit" her Fifth Amendment welcomed
acid her Fifth Amendment does everyone just great.
E.g., United States Apfelbaum, 445 U.S. doesn't begin to placate
sock her "exculpatory no"
doesn't dine with many singles
her taking is sock health without using unenthusiastic thorns
queen "pile on" on yes with help
her blurring grip, an odd, undressed Congress.

Your verdict must be based solely and exclusively on the evidence in the case. You may not be governed by passion, prejudice, sympathy, or any motive whatsoever except a fair and impartial consideration of the evidence.

In other words, don't tamper with the grammar.

If facts are empty masks
or velvet robes

Must we give ourselves over to an astounding belief in completion

Or can a new grammar of decision
defy execution*

And propose more useful scenarios

*"The Supreme Court will hear the case of Daryl Atkins, a Virginia death row inmate with mental retardation, to consider whether executing those with mental retardation offends society's 'evolving standards of decency' and thus violates the Eighth Amendment's ban on cruel and unusual punishment" (Associated Press, 9/25/01).

Summaries

EARLS OF SALISBURY, NORTHHAMPTON AND NOTTINGHAM v. GARNET

Argued: 1606

Garnet, a Catholic priest learned through Catesby about the Gunpowder Plot. It was understood that if the plot was ever discovered, Garnet could reveal the truth. After the plot was discovered, Garnet was arrested. At his trial he truthfully told the details that he knew and was then executed at the west end of Old St. Paul's, 3 May, 1606. Garnet was author of a scholarly treatise on the art of equivocation.

and

UNITED STATES v. NIXON

Argued: 1974

The District Court, upon the motion of the special prosecutor, issued a subpoena to the president requiring him to produce certain tapes and documents relating to precisely identified meetings between the president and others. President Nixon released edited transcripts of some of the subpoenaed conversations, but his counsel filed a "special appearance" and moved to quash the subpoena on the grounds of executive privilege. The Burger court stated that he must yield to the need for that evidence. Jaworski was special prosecutor. Nixon was represented by James St. Clair. Rehnquist, then a junior member, excused himself from this case because he had been a former aide to Watergate defendant John Mitchell.

Procedure: Duel of Equivocations

Garnet: I am bound to keepe the secrets of confession, and to disclose nothing that I heard in Sacramentall confession.

Earle of Nottingham: If one confessed this day to you that to morrow morning he meant to kill the King with a dagger; must you conceal it?

Garnet: I must conceal it.*

Marshall: What, in any of these tapes, is involved in the impeachment proceedings?

Jaworski: What it really narrows down to is a somewhat simple but very important issue in the administration of criminal justice. And that is whether the president, in a pending prosecution, can withhold material evidence from the court, merely on his assertion that the evidence involves confidential communications.

Earle of Salisbury: I desire the libertie of you to aske you some questions of the nature of Confessions?

Garnet: You may my lord, and I will answer you as well as I can.

*"A Bronx man was freed from prison yesterday by a federal judge who said that he never would have been convicted of murder if the jury had known 13 years ago that a guilt-racked teenager had admitted committing the crime to a priest . . . " (*New York Times*, 7/25/01, page 1)

Marshall: What, in any of these tapes, is involved in the impeachment proceedings?

Earle of Salisbury: . . . there needs no secrecie . . . He professed no penitencie, and therefore you could not absolve him

[*To this Garnet denyed to answere, by which the hearers might see his mind.*]

Justice Marshall: Slightly judicial.

St. Clair: Entirely judicial.

Marshall: And that's what's before us?

St. Clair: And that we moved to quash.

Marshall: What, in any of these tapes, is involved in the impeachment proceedings?

Garnet, *faintly*: I might not disclose it to any, because it is a matter of secret confession and would endanger the life of divers men.

Burger: The very integrity of the judicial system and public confidence in the system depend on full disclosure of all the facts within the framework of the rules of evidence.

Earle of Northampton: The matter of Confession, which before you refused to confesse, because you would save lives, you confessed it now to endanger your owne life, and therefore your former answere was idle and frivolous.

St. Clair:	My learned brother has approached this case, I think, in a traditional point of view . . .
Earle of Nottingham:	If one confessed this day to you that to morrow morning he meant to kill the King with a dagger; must you conceal it?
Garnet:	I might not disclose it to any, because it was matter of secret confession and would endanger the life of divers men.
Jaworski:	Now the president may be right in how he reads the Constitution. But he may also be wrong. And if he is wrong, who is there to tell him so? If he is the sole judge, and he is in error in his interpretation, then he goes on being in error in his interpretation.
Justice Stewart:	Well, then this Court will tell him so. That's what this case is about, isn't it?
Jaworski:	Well, that's what I think the case is about, yes, sir.

AUTHORITIES: A LECTURE, including A REAL LIFE DRAMA

> Determined to eliminate any mysterious entity such as life, he insisted on deriving the motion of the heart from known physical processes; in doing so, he turned the heart into a teakettle.
>
> —Richard Westfall, *The Construction of Modern Science*

What is the relation of the line to the self? Fishing line, clothesline, don't forget your lines, a family line, the equator, a tightrope, the border and edge, a vein, a sentence. The line is that which "humanizes" imagination; it forms a ledge so that we won't fall into the "bottomless." Distance simultaneously bound to the ordinary with authority. Authority instigates distances and distance is crucial to the maintenance of the line. A sentence (the line)(the body) is the link between two spaces; it is that which is the overcoming of sides. In its apparent drive toward fragmentation it succeeds in conveying the stance of an object, a material. Why the need for an object in the guise of a life or writing?

> Recollection of the lifeless form of a pyramid or of the suppression of life that is manifested, for instance, in Byzantine mosaics tells us at once that here the need for empathy, which for obvious reasons always tends toward the organic, cannot possibly have determined artistic volition. Indeed, the idea forces itself upon us that here we have an impulse directly opposed to the empathy impulse, which seeks to suppress precisely that in which the need for empathy finds its satisfaction.
>
> —Wilhelm Worringer, *Abstraction and Empathy*

"The OED says that geography is the autobiography of the earth. Or was it geology?"

The floor has many ledges. The foot, unnoticed, captures the space of a crevice by way of a fall. Some of the floors are covered with moss. Why do you write in sentences? Is it necessary for speech, for capturing a space? The rocks lean against each other in various degrees of dependence. Pockets of cold air throw themselves here and there. You may be afraid to turn the corner. You know that no one is there and yet you can imagine someone to be there. This person populates the entire place. Follow the markers. Or follow the person around the corner who is gone when you finally look. The floor. The paths that run beneath the floor. The floor is actually a prop: writing in sentences. Deep holes that scatter through it. If you don't look, you might fall through the floor into a crevice, an angle between two rocks. Cold air hits your side, pushes you here and there.

Streets of townhouses, no alleyways, no corridors. Townhouses are walls with windows shut. A man, a cowboy, an urban waif. In the street, the twelve year olds carry guns. They carry butcher knives to school. A man, a cowboy, walks down the street. He takes out a gun and shoots out all the windows. A million red and yellow arrows. Inside, the occupants sit close to the back wall. Later, outside, they finger the holes in their houses. Now there's a storm in the tall grasses. A man, a cowboy, changes (loses?) his mind. In the storm he's lost all of his senses. He clings to the walls of a darkened shack. So take him back into the city, where his actions are cognizant: taking a knife to school. Recognizing responsibility, a line from the past to the present, from behind a mask of madness. He said:

> *If thou wilt weep my fortunes, take my eyes.*
> *I know thee well enough; thy name is Gloucester.*
> *Thou must be patient; we came crying hither.*
> *Thou know'st the first time that we smell the air*
> *We wawl and cry.*

What is a character witness?

---

praise lacks gold
never lacked frail deed
gives me hills of seas

In an essay on Othello, Kenneth Burke describes Iago as Katharma. Katharmata:

It was the custom at Athens,
lexicographers inform us, to reserve
certain worthless persons, who in case of
plague, famine, or other visitations from
heaven, were thrown into the sea . . . in
the belief that they would cleanse away
or wipe off the guilt of the nation.
—Perspectives on Incongruity

Someone tells me that according to a poetics of difference, there is a need to leave the experimental behind: writers not privileged by the dominant discourse "cannot leave judgement to 'chance.'" But what if the nature of judgment itself is a matter of chance? In winter, 1993, Chief Justice William Rehnquist announced the Supreme Court decision that "innocence is not a constitutional claim." A man on death row, decided guilty in a fair jury trial *is* guilty, even when (as happened in the case that brought forth the opinion), the *real* guilty party is exposed later on.

---

attendants duck increased comforts
citadel violence first lov'd
courtesy too loud

In other words, The Fugitive would still have been put to death for his wife's murder if his time to prove himself innocent had run out. And as far as I can tell, it ran out. "Judgment"—"justice" is a matter of system. Experimental forms are not relinquishing judgment, so much as they are questioning the system that produces such forms of justice, throwing it into new light.

The presence of Iago questions the flawed system. He goes beyond the stance of a necessary evil, a tool for ultimately attaining (through his discard) a cathartic utopian state for the spectator. He is, in fact, a part of that "utopian" state. He can never be totally purged; he is the scene which allows for Othello (and our understanding of Othello/ourselves) to exist at all. We are meant to empathize with (see ourselves as) Othello. But Othello and Iago are "two parts of one fascination" (says Burke). The system of Aristotelian tragedy does not account for the continued presence of Iago in ourselves. An awareness of Iago's systematic/systemic presence necessitates a redefinition of a "utopia" if the utopic result is contingent on Iago's supposed discard.

---

meet me measure of lawn
I would do such a wrong

I have voiced disappointment over this Court's obvious eagerness to do away with any restriction on the States' power to execute whomever and however they please. . . . I have also expressed doubts about whether in the absence of such restrictions, capital punishment remains constitutional at all. . . . Of one thing, however, I am certain. Just as an execution without adequate safeguards is unacceptable, so too is an execution when the condemned prisoner can prove that he is innocent. The execution of a person who can show that he is innocent comes perilously close to simple murder.

—Supreme Court Justice Blackmun, *Herrera vs. Texas*, 1993

---

willow usage good night
good night
cut my leg in two
who is it who cried?

This city was chosen for its prominent doctors. H.H. Richardson used maple around the windows and doors. Who still inhabits this place? "I hope no one is afraid of dead pigeons" he said in the tower that was six stories high. (Six stories of nothing.) A thin ladder reaches high out of sight. A square of height reveals another square like a mirror game. He doesn't touch on the psychology behind the architecture, although it's clear that attitudes have changed. In the hallway, each step crackles with fallen paint. There is a wheelchair. Symmetrical doors reveal similar rooms. Does the paint protect the wood? Or is there a fear of it? Is this fear related to the twin towers and the logic behind their construction? Riddled with bullets. You build a place that people fear to go. In approaching the building, there is no option but to picture yourself being forced into its corners, against the walls of a darkened shack.

The presence of Iago is the experimental. It is the contained within a container that cannot make room for its presence. The character of Iago has always caused me great discomfort. In Orson Welles' film *Othello*, one of the first images is of Iago being forced into a square cage which is then foisted up over the city. He's left to dangle there. There is no moment when "justice has been done," of "finality" (to use Justice Rehnquist's term). When Othello finally asks for a reason behind Iago's perfidy, Iago responds

> *Demand me nothing, what you know, you know,*
> *From this time forth I never will speak word.*

He refuses to become intelligible. And yet it is his unintelligibility that prevents him from finally being discarded. The presence of Iago actually *prevents* the cathartic response for which the play is so often used as an exemplum. He cannot be "thrown into the sea"; he is a corpsed genre (substantial) that shifts the focus, moves the angle, turns monologue into dialogue. Judgment and purgation are no longer applicable in his discussion.

Rain smashes through the paragraph. The weather lifts from one end of the spectrum to the other, all in the course of a day. Why write in sentences? I gave the wrong answer. Geometry will help. Guns change architecture, in that the space used to be open and now there is a confusing series of doors. Also, Frederick Law Olmsted envisioned a city connected by green areas. This has to do with the sentence. To see "I" and "you" as cardboard figures waiting to entertain, to draw in a crowd. The paint crackled with each step and somebody had scrawled up on the hospital wall: "gas, food, lodging." Arrows point in various directions: red and yellow. Lodge in the similar rooms and then you will be similar. However, if the "I" is attached to myself waiting to speak, this might be mistaken as a language of statement. I'm not saying this.

---

chrysolitic sense

---

of why he needs our audience

The written creates vectors that steer like spotlights into various points
of the eye.
Auditory genres grasped then tempted.
The law not to be mixed in future.
The authority of a less legitimate order.
Do not question a genre; the limit between an odd citation.
Who, for example, must be "mixed"?
Transgression belongs to the law.
If something might invite myself from me, the possibility would
separate
two bodies.
Division holds no doubt.
Edges appear to demonstrate the sentences.
The relationship barely tempted from recounting myself.
Majority opinion of sound.
Solving a conflict of definition was never the intention of detail.
Focus on this.
A man shot four times while riding down the hill.
The state of anchors laid out, cables and bags of coal in the run.
To demonstrate this with primary texts in a modest manner at
the edge
of history.

The figure on the left is using the primitive form
in which human muscle power forces
a cutting against the rotation;
the relaxed man on the right
is using rhetorical speech.
The speech is titled:

A REAL LIFE DRAMA (FOUND POEM)

In a spirited argument
eight of nine justices fired questions
but the discussion ranged from goats and butterflies to koalas and even rare bugs splattered on car windshields

Scalia: "Couldn't we pick an uglier example than a
koala bear?"

Scalia: "To say this is taking an animal seems to me just weird."

Souter: "It seems to me you're wrong when you say it's got to be purposeful."

Justice Thomas was the only court member who refrained.

Stevens: "Would I be violating the law if I built a golf course without the intention of causing a bird to become extinct, but with the full knowledge that it would result in the bird's becoming extinct?"

Souter: "Fairness cannot be stretched to the point of calling this a fair trial."

Scalia: *a blistering dissent.*

Stevens: "The right to remain anonymous may be abused when it shields fraudulent conduct. But political speech by its nature will sometimes have unpalatable consequences."

Stevens: "Anonymity is a shield from the tyranny of the majority."

Scalia: "It facilitates wrong by eliminating accountability, which is ordinarily the very purpose of anonymity."

Rehnquist: "This they cannot do without seriously undercutting the orderly process of law."

a spirited argument

Stevens: "The law was nothing more than an attempt to blindfold the public"

Scalia: "[the doctrine] is a structural safeguard establishing high walls and clear distinctions because low walls and vague distinctions will not be judicially defensible in the heat of interbranch conflict."

Scalia: "In dictatorships of the modern world bills of rights are a dime a dozen."

"imperial Presidency" "runaway Congress" "unelected judiciary"

Scalia this week borrowed from poet Robert Frost in offering one of his reasons why: "Good fences make good neighbors."

strongly worded opinion

Stevens: "To engage in such pure speculation while condemning (the) assertion of increased punishment as 'speculative' seems to me not only unpersuasive but actually perverse."

Both lawyers were peppered with questions from eight justices. Only Justice Thomas did not ask one.

Scalia: "They weren't there to recreate. They were there to express something."

O'Connor: "If a circus holds a parade 'expressing no viewpoint except the circus is in town and everybody come,' can an animal rights group demand the right to march in that parade to protest the use of circus animals?"

Stevens: ". . . how to distinguish between a sign for identification and a sign for advocacy?"

Kennedy: ". . . for a Court to tell a private entity how to celebrate is antithetical to the first amendment."

O'Connor: "[your argument is] so far-fetched it's hard to bring this down to reality, down to the real world."

Only Justice Thomas, who remains silent in most arguments, appeared troubled by the notion that the Klan's white cross is a religious symbol.

Thomas: "You say this is a religious symbol. What is the religion of the Klan? . . . If someone said the Klan was carrying a cross down Pennsylvania Avenue, would the average person, a reasonable person think that the Klan was engaging in the free exercise of religion or a political statement?"

impassioned dissents

O'Connor: "You come here arguing for this remarkable proposition to suppress speech in a discriminatory fashion."
Thomas: "What does a burning cross symbolize? . . . Some might see fire in that cross."
O'Connor: "Does a reasonable person know how to read?"

Justice Scalia was also scathing.

Breyer: "Has the paper been piling up?"

Thomas, who came to the Supreme Court under a cloud
and immediately withdrew into a shell of silence,
peppered a lawyer with questions.

THEATER ARRAY

JURY

The effect of this body mechanism (*Körpermechanik*) (in circus performance and athletic events, for example) arises essentially from the spectator's astonishment or shock at the potentialities of his own organism as demonstrated to him by others. This is a subjective effect.

—Laszlo Moholy-Nagy, "Theater, Circus, Variety"

A staged spectacle which consists of a series of placards shooting down on wires hung like crooked tightropes across the ceiling. Somebody has printed on the placards. There is a judge and a jury. A movie queen and a messenger.

~

Swivel chairs and an audience SOMEONE AT A TABLE HIS OR HER THOUGHTS AMPLIFIED FROM ABOVE nominal disbelief as to the events that have occurred between us a messenger in greek garb in the middle of the SKIDS the room a movie queen stands over the letter writer and CHANGES COP CAP over his or her shoulder in the configuration of recent events it seems appropriate we quit ourselves of this outstanding obsession and WINCE back into a productive function therefore meet me at 10 p.m. in the plaza bring all necessary implements by which we will you won't regret it the letter folded and HANDED TO THE MESSENGER THE MOVIE QUEEN FOLDS

●

hammer of the gavel, then

cue card: "WOOD"

speech: Looks out on a blue road; wood as a road, a slate of wood. How did I once have room for an extension at the elbow. Was it then easier to form letters, the messenger asks. First the ground shifted, as did the inner workings. The workings of me, the character. The character assumes the plot and is self-assured at any point of the staging. The wall of the house, wooden siding, is a wall of roads. Spots herself inside, an illness. A retreat into the house.

cue: **"GAVEL"**

sung:

what skin is in the drama
horrible kin and more before him
see the malady fortune has schooling
and then distress unrest

how heavy the aspect of new sense
thus long, the occupants murmuring

it's all alone perchance a piece
of ever seeming new sound grime

now aging capacity of withheld ability
how long? a year? close a door
betwixt thyself you holding it closer
with a key and me for an aspect gone

perchance a piece of turning over
replica gallant miter swing
    not so caught within
    an opinion

●

hammer of the gavel, then

cue card: **"ARM"**

speech: The night is morning to borrow a way of seeming. Now the arm is right. No longer metal in it. When it alights. In front of those who are sleeping, the night is not morning. Point out the window at this: what kind of place to be without? For anything wrong? Moving from one spot to another, it's like a current running from your spine. Split into spaces. Now, let's remind ourselves of caricature. In caricature, we can literally lose the parts of our body. What is considered / separated out as / the central current of yourself—your spine—forms a concentrate at the surface. A painted face swims to the top. Is this the way to know the person who is now gone. Once the person is gone, you wonder what kind of place is this to be without. A painted company. A melodrama.

cue: **"TARGET"**

action: ejection of ribbon fills the floor with
stumbling ribbons
the walks, the badly talks
a place to govern an entire city
with a body to pieces
fine and perfect so go there, see it spread
the old face closes over the new face like a door
falls away like a husk
the street collapses into a grave
cut rinse eye switch
into columnar spacious face

●

hammer of the gavel, then

cue card: **"WOOD"**

speech: That is the relation to Nature. All of the stolen goods laid neatly on the open stair. You count what is missing and don't pay attention to what is there. The argument of a logger. Wood, pristine, swimming through the first dream. A dream without center is an impossibility. It is impossible to know the center of a dream. And so the log floats over the edge. Now the water is clear, the sleeper at rest, the dreams like wickets spread across it. No idea of paying a piper. Unless striking with a mallet is paying a piper.

~

the messenger swings a can and swings that too from his opposite hand's finger skeletons ALL THE WALKING IS beautifully SYNCHRONIZED A small CART WHEELS THROUGH the street messenger placed a rib or other bone within it uplifting SLOW HAPPY DANCE places his gun and cane in it as if at a podium delivering a political speech in the configuration of recent events it seems CROWD SOUNDS RECEDE gradually that we quit ourselves from an overwhelming roar sit down which she can barely shout over until there is absolute silence in WHISPERING sit down

●

hammer of the gavel, then

cue card: "SPAIN ALIBI"

alibi: The two narrowly on a bus to the height of the road where everyone appears to be carrying bread. In the middle of the hill to sit in a doorway, these are two men speculating an accent. It is unclear whether to walk up or down, later discovering that every direction eventually leads to a center square where I soon lay down and lose my head. The speeches get rumpled. To chart it all down I draw a map, key determined by symbols I find in the room where I sleep. Stumble out, lost again on the few streets there might be, suddenly not sure they actually do all lead to the center. There are no women here so I must wear this disorienting disguise which I thought of cleverly, from a movie, while I first passed out on that bench back there. It is so convincing that you mistake me for a salesman. The authentic vendors smack at the back of my knees and I am unable to come up with the proper response. At the edge of the market you insist on snapping a photo at arm's length even though the twisted figures of a thousand vendors are quickly making headway in our direction. You tell me the jangling of the key to the map will give us away and to "simmer down."

cue: "MY NOTES"

he clubs the ground with his boot and this movement
light refraction instead of paint
does it repeat towards the hills
to gauge human measure or private status
instantly applied in each other?
take dusk out of the yoke
and walls fall in
transport such as a turnstile
merges the tear with the spoke
an aperture places everything back, all back in the roping
leather tallow near the cuff
to the place between the slats and buckles
to go on as a clue
a face leans in a direction
objection
click
aperture in the morning
go on
an apparition of what is less fit
the burr spins circular against the metal skin for transport
the gull creeps into the water and settles beneath the wing
keeps the shadow clean
how?
how one puts it together, leading one to the other to the other

cue card: "SPAIN"

speech: I might like to read a map

if every face is a wind that keeps the land
locked to the sea   a copperplate and
signature
on every side   twigged rivers
carry the
blood of them
to include me   with ornament and
frame
a bitter grid
of dismayed
lost populace
how is the place founded by its name
rife with bloomered men strumming lutes
the cartographer's world
peering in
sketching out
into the globe   as it were a moon
constellates his eye   with a roguish ensign
memory alleviates the shallow vine of slogans
how and why I might choose to read a map

somite leads to metamere or
soma: there's more at somat
somat: there's more at thumb
there's not much at thumb
turn back
has the whole crowd of us been deceived?
particles are for exiles
furry scraps
it is more than coincidence
that locks memory to the land
and the present moment to the sea

its intentions
its false relationships

I can't deny my suspicions of the river

we were made to travel on wire
shortages take over and inhabit respiration
as with a lasso
a city disappears into our breath

it bothers us,
a floor protected by the uniform of a ceiling
in other words, ourselves
as rapid air between two tall hands

we know the sea is a table of bottles
that remember the sweet sea
and a fence is against that
which a body breaks
against it

~

The stage will consist of an aluminum proscenium, the action populated by quarrels; which side first, which word slides, the decision finally arbitrary, the maps fold into their faulty developments causing the lands that we find to be distorted, flexed into an accordian to make room for more alluring captivities.

Will the audience tire easily? How might this affect sentencing? Who will fall dumb? First, the placards serve as a reminder, a sort of leap or troop leader. But as they proceed to fall they cause traffic . . . unreasonable visual tricks. Parts of the body are separated, rearranged, and reassigned according to verdict.

~

Perhaps a sound that "tune" causes a circle to close in to CLOSE IN ON HIS EYES so as to see so behind them I can't believe I can't believe you're FLASHBACK behind the darkening eyes to starlet SINGING at dawn a prelude or two an ordinary healthy guy in cop cap on fog street takes you through two preludes to dawn then CIRCLES BACK behind them speaking you can see them speaking deliberately NOT LOOKING BACK because memory I can't believe you're closing in the fog street CHANGE OF SCENE with a line sliding across the screen to make good to be good for ten bucks and a flashback so as to see

cue: **"PORTRAIT"**

the first petitioner
reveals

yes, on the basis of proof
there is in fact an eyewitness
of coherence and unity
a general neatening
as it were

however,
the conviction misleads
those outside the segment
of truth
that all has been taken care of

those originally judged
are given their own rooms
as opposed to being welcomed
into the room that has abandoned them
that is a slaying of sorts
that is celebrated

actual innocence does not entitle relief

~

Now the place is becoming more recognizable. Those sitting before me are not an audience at all, but waiting for an outcome.

~

cue: "ANATOMY"

as substance strains into categories   thinking's chain

of events   bread, a reasonable symptom

all roots disorder   humours   pleasant at first

various gout and continual fear   in mind

black jaundice   oil, vinegar, wine

why are they so fearful   hate light, crudity of heart

to offer violence to the self sings in the ears

innate heat in which the diagnosis clocks habits

of body and head   frenzy, ecstasy, fear of air

cue: **"MY NOTES"**

dear X
that there is inscription
on the inside of my voice
          marks visual parts
through attachment I can see you
notes I build between us
          lack alignment

a little noise, a photograph
a recounting back of instance
winces
          spacing needs adjustment
behind a tomb
the five white stones
the small landscape
the next landscape
          national

it is difficult to intrude a depth
as is possible in the process of printing
where there are always letters forming
despite their suppression
where is the music where is the breath where is
the line, etc.

●

bang of the gavel, then

cue card: "ANATOMY"

speech: The split sides are explained in simultaneous translation of the day's events, this house is the only place where I am free. A speech is my house. Trying to capture me inside a conversation, I resist, I am off into the morning and wake heavily. Sides resting on the interior as a tent is intent on its center. There are other voices all through it and handwriting I cannot recognize. Freedom in a container, although the contents rearrange. From "pent" because it has five ingredients. All are deadly. You can be happy here, I was told. As long as you wear this. Don't run away from a debt. You can be happy in summer in a state of torpor. There is a lot of nostalgia in this body. Not to be confused with melancholy and its numerous petitions. Where the words come from, where they go is contingent on (the housing of the discarded) you.

cue: "ANATOMY"

bread flesh herbs

too coarse to be eaten parts: heads, feet

pigeons of herbs preparing sharp sauces

causes of unnatural things
irascible

pleasant at first tending to evil guts

in the vinegar fog delight the appetite blind

if cold, ambition marks a mad spark

hot and grievous symptom of prophet vision

wanders all over the body and home in the dark

~

returning the luck returning THE WIRE ACROSS THE NECK and back beneath the door I know you I've heard of your temper and now's the time for every discontent to meet back in the body onto the paper do you hear that sound as an escape from a temper or was there ever more to meet the ear by now far away perhaps and causes a stir and DISCONTENTED SNARL doesn't like him or his body gives in to all symptoms that combine into a species of thought and dream dry body continual fear HE DOESN'T DARE in a question to he who doesn't like or dream to meet discontent far away from the wires of melancholy in body and mind no GREAT SIGN OF RAIN but damp hands of solicitude TOSS ALL OUT time and again

~

You follow a person through a variety of routines until you feel he/she is a close friend. Only to see in a photograph or other staging device that they are wearing a debilitating mask that keeps the stranger clean. Now the stranger is strange and you focus back on the placards. Unlike a character, a word doesn't suffer as dissembler. You don't feel cheated.

~

Glance thorough glance at numerous feet and calves as they NAVIGATE THE MUD puddles the presence of a wall is numerous as are the shopping THEY ARE SHOPPING for small things each person might have ten such things to sell SELLING at the mud puddle market the messenger is quite sure HE SEES a witness although always it is HIS FEET his feet are in the glance that slips down into the sky THE APPEAL the sky in the puddles.

~

THE CHARACTER

It was a fair trial. The body proves the process and the animal shows its wool. This is an idea that allows for immediate access. The fair was not a trial, but a place to show the animals. The man was an animal, and thus his trial was fair.[1] This is not an aesthetic sphere. The equation shifts as analogical contexts reach out and shake the snowflakes over the dome of the city.

see a world salute a sir
who sets a table
and sues the national object
and kills and keels and
bloodies the tent
the hand that pours judicial seizure[2]

detachment, there's order; order is the fruit of action[3]

---

1 Can we really fault the Russian director Meyerhold for not mentioning the Russian fairground, but instead placing all of his attention on French and Italian models?[a]

2 The proceedings were complex and required intense concentration; however, N.L. and I found our attention wandering to the man who filled the water pitchers that were placed before the justices. He wore lime green slacks.

3 Action or animation? It is possible to perceive animation in a completely inactive subject—even in a subject that is dead.[b] There is no perception without attachment.

---

a can we fault *you* for delimiting the justice system within an aesthetic sphere?

b "Attachment is a manufacturer of illusions and whoever wants reality ought to be detached."—Simone Weill

this suspect sets a table of fatality[4]

Innocence applies to the character in the way that fine china applies to a whale. At least in the eyes of the many rides that trauma the body on its way up and down. Amusements: perhaps you've seen him?[5] The lines in his hands coincide with the lines on which you wait hour after hour, at the end of which you cash in your ticket and fall up and into the sky. The gavel always strikes him, it strikes him now and again.[6]

a jeer
over part of necessity
I
pull past the fair outerly
past an action.
might a sort of passivity
agitate action?[7]

---

4 My point exactly
5 Meyerhold writes: "In [the director's] attempts to reproduce reality 'as it really is,' he improves the puppets further and further[c] until finally he arrives at a far simpler solution to the problem: replace the puppets with real men."[d]
6 See Bill Irwin's "The Courtroom"
7 "We want receiving centers for dots and dashes"—H.D.

---

c in other words, the actors
d in other words, the character

"a rest, sit close a while
the sick, the contrary
the following that I speak of
a rest, they'll have a rest"[8]

You purchase a future. It has nothing to do with bars or weights or balance. Look at your punishment as a purchase.[9]

the author of himself's complication

so that one plus one and he
one plus one and he[10]

effort to withhold
a so-called someone in the hold of the boat
the sail as contract
sinking environment[11]

the guard did order
superior orders, infinitely under
put over the other sea sea green
grainy, etc.
contact the circle tangent to discretion
let them know we are here
to enter society

---

8 For indeed they must rest. The costumes she had designed for them treated the body as an axis from which their limbs could only pivot.

9 Emerson wrote: "The least change in our point of view gives the whole world a pictorial air. A man who seldom rides, needs only to get into a coach and traverse his own town, to turn the street into a puppet-show."

10 "Do not presume too much upon my love; I may do that I shall be sorry for."[e]

11 "A ship is a habitat before being a means of transport . . . the enjoyment of being enclosed reaches its paroxysm when, from the bosom of this unbroken inwardness, it is possible to watch, through a large window-pane, the outside vagueness of the waters, and thus define, in a single act, the inside by means of its opposite." —Roland Barthes[f]

---

e in other words, Cassius

f see "Cabins" by Max Beckmann

"Knock, knock; never at quiet!
What are you?"[12]

the good me, more
a part pieced across the storm
I
leave a mark
on the destructed
hillock bound

I swear it
I crossed over and then
I fell in

"do you play what the others play
at the beach
by the water
in the core?"[13]

12 I've seen this porter portrayed as a vaudevillian. "Anon, anon! I pray you, remember the porter."[g] Laughter is the societal urge, yet laughter is also that which is most aberrant.

13 The character said this in his sleep.[h]

g in other words, Macbeth

h or was it you?

The essay is not another thing:
the mis-knowing of the man
is there
The guilty, even his story
is proof of experiments
of conscience[14]

that power is something,
she thinks

whereby a reader is pushed from the page[15]

continuous assault
of fuss

14 Or of annotation.
15 {turn page over a couple of times very exagerratedly}[i]

i {turn page over a couple of times very exagerratedly}

poor attendant detached from
that to be attended, misfortune,
misfortune suffices not
he fights consolation, the
attendant[16]

there we meet our friend[17]

good resides in us inasmuch
as good exists in anything
the hourly thought I thank you sir
and sit down father
rest you—[18]

---

16 Is that related?[j] I have to agree with you there.[k] I'm not sure
17 In other words, the character.
18 I would like to talk—

---

j it seemed a bit frivolous to me.
k why don't we chat like this more often?

across destruction it is light
not the consolation—love—
it is light
a self transported from letters
into things, the letters themselves
sir, speed you;
what's your will?—[19]

attachment succeeds in an interior
however, illusory;
in this place resides a city
and within resides the border skeleton
our eye skids the steel wall of it[20]

"Then there's life in't."

"Sa, sa, sa, sa."[21]

---

19 I actually have something I'd like to say—
20 But I've lost my notes.[l]
21 King Lear comes back to the surface, and admits that he knows Gloucester.[m]

---

l don't you recognize me? can't you see me? your voice sounds so familiar . . .
m but will he acknowledge me?

TO THE READER

There's a voice in the room and what are you noticing. What are the sounds in the room. Is there a bell that says that the dinner is ready to be served. Is there a bird warming up outside that you are noticing. In what ways does that noticing mean anything good. Is this its own performance or part of something else. Are you listening to someone's voice while reading this to yourself. Are you listening to the words that the voice sounds or simply to the sound. What kind of sound are you hearing beyond the voice that's sounding. Do you hear the cars on the road. Do you hear the hum of the fan on the floor. Do you hear anything from the hallway or from the rooms next door. Do you hear the one voice whispering to the other. Do you hear the chairs scraping against the floor. Do you hear a door closing and a latch latching. Do you hear the sound of the breath of the person next to you. Are you noticing your own body as it sits in the chair that may or may not be comfortable. Do you find yourself slowing down, looking up, tracking back.

Are you following words that are sounded and trying to situate yourself in relation to them. Are the words the wallpaper that surround the true activity of someone sitting up straight in front of you and you admire that person's coat or hairstyle or the meal that they have ordered. Do you feel that the words are about you simply because of a pronoun, or is empathy outside of grammar. Are there clues in a text like a hand intimately clasping. Is the skin there complete sensation. Are there two seeds from an orange on the table.

Does the butterfly serve as some kind of analogy, a quasi-splice for reeving new halyards. Are you noticing. Is this an easy space for capturing your attention. Or is the smoke beginning to get to you. Are you noticing a waver in the over of the edge. Are you noticing a cross-current in the waving having and the come on over here of the wave. Do you wish you had eaten a bit more before reading this. Which tree wavers under the weight of the bird. Did you drop this. Have you forgotten the beginning before my interruption. Does the first person pronoun jar unwelcome and unkind or does it reveal a body that is foreign and only good. Do you remember the aphetic elixir of the waver wavering wave. How straight is your spine. How sharp is your tongue. How is the shoulder, soldier.

Is it a large or small crowd. Would you use the word successful to describe a crowd or a poem. Are you sure you're in the right location. Have the birds started to warm up yet. Are the lyrics to their songs like oo la la. Are you frapping for lashing drumheads and mousing hooks. Are you surging a line on a wince, then jamming a bight of the fall into the upper block. Could this be some kind of bid for a recently vacated cabinet position. Do you marry the two lines, laying them into each other. Are you the clove hitch, the slippery hitch, the stunner hitch, struggling with your own personalized orange revolution. Do you tie the shoe clerk's knot, the bow tie, the mermaid's braid, the bell knot. Have your fingers made even the slightest mark or indentation.

"Target" was the libretto for a vocal composition of the same name, composed by Keeril Makan. It premiered at The Weill Music Institute at Carnegie Hall, October 10, 2004. *Leaflet I* and *Leaflet II* incorporates language taken from leaflets that were dropped on Afghanistan after 9/11. Language for *PsyOps: Know Your Target* was sourced from descriptions of military psychological operations written by a former U.S. Army officer. An extended version of this poem, titled "The Ring of Strategic Influence: A Lecture," was published in the Green Pages (compiled by Adam Pendleton) in *Hey Hey Glossolalia* ed. Mark Beasley (Creative Time Books, 2008).

"The Joker," "The Franklin Party," excerpts from "Financial District," and "Mercury Rising (A Visualization)" were originally published in *The Network*, Fence Books, 2010 (selected for the National Poetry Series by Prageeta Sharma). Thanks to Rebecca Wolff. "The Joker" contains quotations from *Hearings Held Before the Special Committee on the Investigation of the American Sugar Refining Co. & Others,* U.S. Congress, 1911-1912.

Public Figures was published by Wesleyan University Press in 2012. Thanks to Suzanna Tammien. Image of Zouave jacket is from *Godey's Lady's Book*, November 1859. All street and statue photos taken by Jena Osman.

Useful Knowledge: A Genealogy of Shares was commissioned to mark the occasion of the 200th anniversary year of the Philadelphia Athenæum, with support from the Pew Center for Arts and Heritage.

"Dead Text," "Authorities: A Lecture," "A Real Life Drama (Found Poem)" and "The Character" originally published in *The Character*, Beacon Press, 1999. The Emily Dickinson poem in "Dead Text" is from fascicle 31, printed in *The Manuscript Books of Emily Dickinson*, ed. R.W. Franklin, Harvard University Press, 1981. Quotes from Supreme Court arguments in "A Real Life Drama (Found Poem)" were culled from email updates sent from the Legal Information Institute at Cornell Law School in 1998. "Starred Together" was orginally published in *Hambone* (ed. Nathaniel Mackey) and then again in *The Best American Poetry 2002* (Scribner, ed. Robert Creeley).

"Dropping Leaflets," "Press Scrutiny: The Doubles," and "The Astounding Complex" were originally published in *An Essay in Asterisks*, Roof Books, 2004. Thanks to James Sherry. All language in "Dropping Leaflets" was culled from transcripts of press conferences given by President George W. Bush, Vice President Dick Cheney, Defense Secretary Donald Rumsfeld, and Director of Homeland Security Tom Ridge in October 2001. The U.S. Supreme Court summary excerpts in "The Astounding Complex" can be found at http://www.findlaw.com/casecode/supreme.html. The interrogation of Garnet is taken from *A True and Perfect Relation of the Proceedings at the Several Arraignments of the Late Most Barbarous Traitors*, London, 1606.

"Tacit Captions" was originally published in the Summer 2013 issue of *Poetry Northwest*, guest edited by Andrew Zawacki.

"Disclosures" was originally published in the online journal *Poets Reading the News* on July 21, 2018. Some phrases in this poem come from articles by Yale law professor Heather Gerken. Similar to tv ads where politicians have to admit that they "endorse this message," Gerkin and her collaborators propose that ads funded by groups that don't want to reveal their donors must include the text "This ad was paid for by X, which does not disclose the identity of its donors." In the *Washington Post* Gerkin wrote "Given how much of the campaign-finance system the court has eviscerated in recent years, disclosures are becoming the only game in town."

"Falling Down NYC, 19th Century Edition" was originally published in *Supplement* (eds. Ariel Resnikoff and Orchid Tierney), fall 2016. All text sourced from 19th century newspapers. This poem is an homage to Dannielle Tegeder's "Falling Apart NYC," which can be found at https://www.ubu.com/ubu/unpub/Unpub_039_Tegeder.pdf. It was also inspired by Teju Cole's "Small Fates."

"Invention" and parts of "The Periodic Table of Elements as Assembled by Dr. Zhivago, Oculist" were originally published in *The Character*. The latter poem has had many lives and half-lives on-line and was conceived as language to be recombined by the reader. The latest iteration was created by Vladimir Zykov in 2011 and is periodically available at http://vladworld.com/zhivago/. At this point, the periodic table used as a template for the piece is out of date, as more elements have been added. Figure 1 is a screenshot from the movie *Shattered*. Figure 2 is an illustration by Fermin Rocker that accompanied the Henry James story "The Jolly Corner."

"Popular Science" and "System of Display" are from *Motion* Studies (Ugly Duckling Presse, 2019). Thanks to Anna Moschovakis and Matvei Yankelevich. An earlier version of "Popular Science" was published in *Triple Canopy* as part of the "Common Minds" series. Thanks to Lucy Ives. Thanks to Matt Cohen, the Walt Whitman Archive, and Duke Special Collections for Whitman's phrenological report. "System of Display" was written with the help of a Temple University/Wagner Free Institute of Science Humanities & Arts Research Fellowship.

Corporate Relations was published by Burning Deck Press in 2014. Thanks to Keith and Rosmarie Waldrop! The image titled "Graves of the Dead Rocked by Mine Caves" is from "Exhibits in connection with Brief of the City of Scranton, Intervenor" used as evidence in the 1922 case Pennsylvania Coal Company v. Mahon. Composer Ted Hearne set selections from the book to music in his *Sound from the Bench*, which premiered in 2014, performed by The Crossing choir, conducted by Donald Nally. Excerpts here © Ted Hearne.

"Dissent and the Hydra" was selected by Erica Hunt for the Academy of American Poets' Poem-a-Day on July 22, 2022. I started this poem just after Justice Ruth Bader Ginsburg passed away and picked it up again after Justice Samuel Alito's draft opinion, which overturns Roe v. Wade, was leaked to the press. Ginsburg was considered a great dissenter; perhaps her most famous dissent was in Shelby v. Holder in 2013, a ruling that struck down the Voting Rights Act of 1965. This poem is built from language sourced from that case, the Alito draft, and from the definition of "hydra" in the Oxford English Dictionary. I'm interested in how collage can serve as another kind of dissent.

Jury was published as a chapbook by Meow Press (ed. Joel Kuszai) in Buffalo, NY in 1996.

"To the Reader" was published in *Hot Whiskey Magazine* (ed. Michael Koshkin and Jennifer Rogers), Boulder 2006.

Thanks to Amze Emmons, my best reader.

Thanks to Adam Pendleton, Craig Garrett, Jessica Kitz, and Alec Mapes-Frances for making this very large array happen. The real Very Large Array is a giant radio telescope observatory located in a volcanic field in central New Mexico.

Jena Osman
A Very Large Array: Selected Poems

Designed by Alec Mapes-Frances

DABA
68 Washington Avenue
Brooklyn, NY 11205
dabapress.net

Distributed by
ARTBOOK | D.A.P.
75 Broad Street, Suite 630
New York, NY 10004
www.artbook.com

Printed by die Keure in Belgium

DABA 010
ISBN 978 1 7346817 9 6